THE DAWN OF HEAVEN BREAKS

THE DAWN OF

heaven

BREAKS

Anticipating eternity

Edited by SHARON JAMES

EVANGELICAL PRESS

EVANGELICAL PRESS

Evangelical Press
Faverdale North, Darlington, DL3 0PH England
Evangelical Press USA
P. O. Box 825, Webster, NY 14580 USA
email: sales@evangelicalpress.org
www.evangelicalpress.org

First published 2007

Unless otherwise indicated, Scripture quotations are from the Holy Bible, New International Version. Copyright © 1973, 1978, 1984, International Bible Society. Used by permision of Hodder & Stoughton, a member of the Hodder Headline Group. All rights reserved.

British Library Cataloguing in Publication Data available
ISBN-13 978 0 85234 641 9   ISBN 0 85234 641 7

PRINTED AND BOUND IN GREAT BRITAIN

*Dedicated with love and gratitude to
the church family at Emmanuel*

BLEST BE the tie that binds
our hearts in Christian love;
The fellowship of kindred minds
is like to that above.

From sorrow, toil, and pain,
and sin we shall be free;
And perfect love and friendship reign
through all eternity.

~ JOHN FAWCETT ~

Contents

xi   Acknowledgements
xiii Introduction

Anticipating heaven

2   'I will raise them up at the last day'
3   'Whoever comes to me, I will never drive away'
4   The Saints' Everlasting Rest
6   Living in the light of eternity
8   'It is well with my soul'
10 Absolute assurance

Times of illness and pain

14 God's presence with his people in times of pain
15 God is our treasure
16 Physical healing is not always the will of God
18 'O Joy, that seekest me through pain'
20 'Set me free from my prison'
21 Suffering and glory
22 Outwardly wasting away — inwardly being renewed
23 God's providence in all things
24 Sleeplessness

26 A patient heart
28 Illness and our spiritual life

Aging

31 The blessings in growing older
32 God's faithfulness throughout life
34 The golden bowl is broken
35 Loneliness — and the unchanging friend
36 Exceeding great and precious promises
38 The triumph of faith
42 Prayer of an elderly Christian: 'You are taking down
    my earthly tent with much tenderness and love'
44 'Abide with me'
47 The loss of memory
50 My journey into Alzheimer's disease
54 'Our God, our help in ages past'
56 My resting place
58 Becoming more like Christ

Facing death

60 Absent from the body, present with the Lord
62 'Underneath are the everlasting arms'
64 'The Sun of righteousness... fills the whole
    hemisphere'
65 'Yet will I fear no ill'
66 The prospect of heaven gives courage in the face
    of death

68 'Alone with none but you, my God'
70 Crossing the river
74 The Lord will provide
76 'Rock of Ages'
78 'We will not fear'
79 'Where, O death, is your sting?'
80 On facing death
82 'Just as I am'
84 I do not fear death
86 A prisoner's dying thoughts
89 Christ – our hope in death
90 'For ever with the Lord'
92 A Passion hymn

And then... eternity

97 The coming of the Lord
98 The coming of the King
101 God will be with them
102 Judgement: the putting right of all wrongs
104 God's gracious purpose for the whole cosmos
106 The biblical hope of bodily resurrection
109 Old Testament prophecies about the new heavens and earth
114 The glories of the renewed universe
116 Will we know each other in the new creation?
118 Continuity in the new creation
120 Service in the new creation
122 'Then, Lord, shall I fully know'

124   Heaven, a world of love
130   'The dawn of heaven breaks'

139   Notes
143   Select bibliography
147   Index

Acknowledgements

My thanks to Phil Roberts, of Tentmaker Publications, for giving me Nearer Home: Comforts and Counsels for the Aged *by William Schenck (published in 1868, and reprinted by Tentmaker Publications in 2003). It was reading* Nearer Home *that inspired me to work on this anthology, and I have included some extracts from that work. Any extracts marked 'anonymous' have been taken from* Nearer Home.

I am very grateful to Janice Van Eck for editing and laying out this book, and also for sending me Charlotte Elliott's Hours of Sorrow Cheered and Comforted.

'Alone with none but you, my God' and 'For ever with the Lord' are quoted with permission from Praise Trust.

I have abridged and modernized some of the older extracts, to make the material more accessible for some readers.

'YOUR SUN will never set again,
  and your moon will wane no more;
The Lord will be your everlasting light.'

~ ISAIAH 60:20 ~

WHEN evening comes, there will be light.

~ ZECHARIAH 14:7 ~

THE SANDS of time are sinking;
  The dawn of heaven breaks:
The summer morn I've sighed for,
  The fair, sweet morn awakes.
Dark, dark hath been the midnight
  But dayspring is at hand
And glory – glory dwelleth
  In Immanuel's land.

~ ANNE ROSS COUSIN ~

Introduction

This anthology gathers together some of the hymns and Bible passages that have been of most comfort to those who are facing illness, aging, and death. It also includes quotations from well loved preachers and authors. As with any anthology, you can dip in and out and read just a section at a time.

If you are reading sections aloud to someone, offer to read the Bible passages from their own Bible if preferred (it can be better, especially for elderly people, to stay with a version they are familiar with).

Who is this book for?

The promises of God are for all those who come to him in faith, believing in his Son the Lord Jesus. 'Whoever comes to me, I will never drive away' (John 6:37). The only qualification is to give up our own efforts to win favour with God. We have to come to him with empty hands, trusting in Christ alone for salvation.

ANTICIPATING *heaven*

'I will raise them up at the last day'

THEN JESUS DECLARED, 'I am the bread of life. He who comes to me will never go hungry, and he who believes in me will never be thirsty. But as I told you, you have seen me and still you do not believe. All that the Father gives me will come to me, and whoever comes to me I will never drive away. For I have come down from heaven not to do my will but to do the will of him who sent me. And this is the will of him who sent me, that I shall lose none of all that he has given me, but raise them up at the last day. For my Father's will is that everyone who looks to the Son and believes in him shall have eternal life, and I will raise him up at the last day.'

~ JOHN 6:35-40 ~

'Whoever comes to me, I will never drive away'

At times of weakness, illness and exhaustion, many Christians lose assurance of salvation and wonder if they really will get to heaven. At such times, we need to remember this great promise: 'whoever comes to me, I will never drive away' (John 6:37). The nineteenth century preacher, Charles Haddon Spurgeon (1834-1892) wrote of this text:

CAN WE NOT ALL COME, just now, and trust Jesus Christ? I mean not only you who have never trusted Christ before, but I would hope that all of us, who have believed in Jesus Christ would begin trusting in him again. I wonder how many times I have had to begin my spiritual life over again at the foot of the cross. I am always doing it, and I am never so happy, so safe, or, I believe, so holy, as when I stand just as I did at first, at the foot of the cross, and look up, and say to my dear Lord and Saviour,

> *Nothing in my hands I bring:*
> *Simply to thy cross I cling.*

~ CHARLES HADDON SPURGEON ~

The Saints' Everlasting Rest

How often do you think about heaven? One of the greatest pastors in church history, Richard Baxter (1615-1691) urged all Christians to set aside time each day to meditate on heaven. His first book was published in 1650, entitled The Saints' Everlasting Rest. *In it, he urged his readers to get alone, and think, and read, and pray:*

Go away into a private place, at a convenient time, and put aside other distractions. Look up towards heaven. Remember that your everlasting rest is there. Meditate on its wonder and reality. Rise from sense to faith, by comparing heavenly with earthly joys, until you are transformed from a forgetful sinner, and a lover of the world, to an ardent lover of God. Meditate on heaven until you are changed from a fearful coward to a resolved Christian. Meditate until your unfruitful sadness is turned to joy. Meditate until your heart is weaned away from earth to heaven, until you are taken up with the delight of walking with God.

You will be as one who stands on the top of a high mountain looking down on the world below: fields, woods, cities and towns will seem like little spots. In fact that is how insignificant all earthly things will now appear! The most powerful rulers will seem as grasshoppers; the busy, contentious, covetous world, will be like a heap of ants. You will not fear the threats of men. You will not be attracted by the honours of the world. Temptations will lose their strong appeal. Afflictions will seem less grievous. Every mercy will be more greatly appreciated. And, by God's grace, it is for you to choose whether you live this blessed life or not!

~ RICHARD BAXTER ~

Living in the light of eternity

Robert Murray M'Cheyne (1813-1843) was only twenty-nine when he died, but his ministry had a profound spiritual impact in Scotland. His friend Andrew Bonar wrote his biography, which soon became a spiritual classic. Bonar's wife Isabella remembered her first meeting with M'Cheyne: 'There was something singularly attractive about Mr M'Cheyne's holiness. It was not his matter nor his manner either that struck me; it was just the living epistle of Christ — a picture so lovely, I felt I would have given all the world to be as he was.' M'Cheyne typically urged his congregation at Dundee:

GO ON DEAR FRIENDS, but an inch of time remains, and then the eternal ages roll on forever; but an inch in which we may stand and proclaim the way of salvation to a perishing world.

One of M'Cheyne's last messages included the following passionate appeal:

> Oh! brethren, be wise. 'Why stand ye all the day idle?' In a little moment it will be all over. A little while and the day of grace will be over – preaching, praying will be done. A little while, and we shall stand before the great white throne – a little while, and the wicked shall not be; we shall see them going away into everlasting punishment. A little while, and the work of eternity shall be begun. We shall be like him – we shall see him day and night in his temple – we shall sing the new song, without sin and without weariness, for ever and ever.

In a letter to a friend he wrote:

> Ah! there is nothing like a calm look into the eternal world to teach us the emptiness of human praise, the sinfulness of self-seeking and vain glory – to teach us the preciousness of Christ, who is called the Tried Stone.

~ ROBERT MURRAY M^cCHEYNE ~

'It is well with my soul'

Horatio G. Spafford (1828-1888) was a wealthy nineteenth-century American businessman. He was also a devout Christian. The Great Chicago Fire of 1871 almost ruined him financially, but he and his wife devoted themselves to ministering to the survivors. In November 1873, the family were due to go together to Europe. Spafford was delayed by business. His wife and four daughters set sail — he was to follow on when he could. Their ship sank. Anna, eleven; Maggie, nine; Bessie, seven; and Tanetta, two, all drowned. His wife survived, and on arrival in England sent the famous telegram: 'Saved, alone.' Spafford set out to join his wife. As his ship crossed the Atlantic and came to the point near where his daughters had drowned, he retreated to his cabin, and penned the following triumphant lines:

WHEN PEACE, like a river, attendeth my way,
  When sorrows like sea billows roll;
Whatever my lot, thou hast taught me to say,
  It is well, it is well, with my soul.

Though Satan should buffet, though trials should come,
  Let this blessed assurance control,
That Christ hath regarded my helpless estate,
  And hath shed his own blood for my soul.

My sin! O the bliss of this glorious thought!
  My sin! not in part, but the whole,
Is nailed to His cross, and I bear it no more,
  Praise the Lord, praise the Lord, O my soul!

For me, be it Christ, be it Christ hence to live!
  If Jordan above me shall roll,
No pang shall be mine, for in death as in life
  Thou wilt whisper thy peace to my soul.

But Lord, 'tis for thee, for thy coming we wait;
  The sky, not the grave, is our goal;
O trump of the angel! O voice of the Lord!
  Blessed hope! Blessed rest of my soul!

And Lord, haste the day when my faith shall be sight,
  The clouds be rolled back as a scroll;
The trump shall resound, and the Lord shall descend,
  Even so, it is well with my soul.

~ HORATIO G. SPAFFORD ~

Absolute assurance

'Now I have found the ground wherein' is a beautiful testimony of Christian assurance. The author, Johann Andreas Rothe (1688-1758) was the Moravian pastor at Berthelsdorf from 1722 to 1737. Count Nicholas von Zinzendorf (1700-1760), the Moravian leader, welcomed religious refugees and built up a thriving Christian community on his estate at Herrnhut, which was part of Rothe's parish. This community became famous for mercy ministries and mission work. John Wesley (1703-1791) translated numerous Moravian hymns from the German. Verse 5 of the hymn alludes to these verses in Habakkuk:

> Though the fig tree does not bud
>   and there are no grapes on the vines,
> though the olive crop fails
>   and the fields produce no food,
> though there are no sheep in the pen
>   and no cattle in the stalls,
> yet I will rejoice in the LORD,
>   I will be joyful in God my Saviour (Habakkuk 3:17-18).

Now I HAVE FOUND the ground wherein
   Sure my soul's anchor may remain —
The wounds of Jesus, for my sin
   Before the world's foundation slain;
Whose mercy shall unshaken stay,
   When heaven and earth are fled away.

Father, thine everlasting grace
   Our scanty thought surpasses far,
Thy heart still melts with tenderness,
   Thine arms of love still open are
Returning sinners to receive,
   That mercy they may taste and live.

O Love, thou bottomless abyss,
   My sins are swallowed up in thee!
Covered is my unrighteousness,
   Nor spot of guilt remains on me,
While Jesus' blood, through earth and skies,
   Mercy, free, boundless mercy! cries.

With faith I plunge me in this sea,
   Here is my hope, my joy, my rest;
Hither, when hell assails, I flee,
   I look into my Saviour's breast:
Away, sad doubt and anxious fear!
   Mercy is all that's written there.

...continued

Though waves and storms go o'er my head,
   Though strength, and health, and friends be gone,
Though joys be withered all and dead,
   Though every comfort be withdrawn,
On this my steadfast soul relies —
   Father, thy mercy never dies!

Fixed on this ground will I remain,
   Though my heart fail and flesh decay;
This anchor shall my soul sustain,
   When earth's foundations melt away:
Mercy's full power I then shall prove,
   Loved with an everlasting love.

~ JOHANN ANDREAS ROTHE ~
TRANSLATED BY JOHN WESLEY

Times of illness and pain

God's presence with his people in times of pain

'FEAR NOT, for I have redeemed you; I have summoned you by name; you are mine. When you pass through the waters, I will be with you; and when you pass through the rivers, they will not sweep over you. When you walk through the fire, you will not be burned; the flames will not set you ablaze. For I am the LORD, your God, the Holy One of Israel, your Saviour.'

~ ISAIAH 43:1-3 ~

BUT HE SAID TO ME, 'My grace is sufficient for you, for my power is made perfect in weakness.' Therefore I will boast all the more gladly about my weaknesses, so that Christ's power may rest on me. That is why, for Christ's sake, I delight in weaknesses, in insults, in hardships, in persecutions, in difficulties. For when I am weak, then I am strong.

~ 2 CORINTHIANS 12:9-10 ~

BUT HE KNOWS the way that I take; when he has tested me I shall come forth as gold.

~ JOB 23:10 ~

God is our treasure

When health and strength are removed, we are reminded that ultimately God himself is our greatest treasure.

YET I AM ALWAYS with you; you hold me by my right hand. You guide me with your counsel, and afterwards you will take me into glory. Whom have I in heaven but you? And earth has nothing I desire besides you. My flesh and my heart may fail, but God is the strength of my heart and my portion for ever.

~ PSALM 73:23-26 ~

Physical healing is not always the will of God

Margaret Clarkson was born in 1915, and suffered ill-health through much of her life. Her first remembered words were 'my head hurts'; she endured migraine headaches as a small child and contracted juvenile arthritis at the age of three. This resulted in severe pain throughout her life. She qualified as a teacher, and taught elementary school for thirty-eight years. She never married, but had numerous 'spiritual children'. She wrote several books and many hymns. Her personal experience of suffering, and the real consolation to be found in the sovereignty of God are reflected in much of her writing.

WHEN PRAYING FOR HEALING, we must remember that from New Testament days right down to the present, God has seen fit to heal some and to withhold healing from others. Paul's 'thorn in the flesh' is a case in point, and the suffering saints of church history bear abundant testimony to the fact that God does not always remove his hedges from the lives of those he loves. We should seek healing, but always undergirding our asking must be our complete acceptance of what God in his sovereign love may see fit to send us. He may say, 'Take up your bed and walk', or he may let the thorns of our hedge press more closely about us... He has promised to save all who come to him in faith for salvation, but I do not find any such all-embracing promise concerning healing.

Great anguish is wrought in souls already overborne by pain when well-meaning but misinformed persons assure the sufferer that he must be deficient in faith, otherwise he would be healed. God may see fit to heal one believing soul and leave another, of equal or even greater faith and devotion, to suffer for years; this is his sovereign prerogative... He may show his strength at an even more critical point – not by healing these sufferers, but by sustaining them in their pain, thus showing Christ's victory by enabling them to triumph over evil even in the midst of it. This is undoubtedly the reason for much unexplained suffering in the lives of God's people. God is working out his mysterious and eternal purposes through us, using our frail, pain-prone bodies to show his wisdom and his grace before earth and hell and heaven for his own glory. Both by healing and by withholding healing, God is glorified (EPHESIANS 1:12) ...

Oh, the release, the freedom of those who suffer according to the will of God and have committed the keeping of their souls to him with the grace of a great acceptance, convinced that God gives only good! Theirs may be the gift of true healing – healing of mind, heart, and spirit – and the peace that the world can neither give nor take away (1 PETER 4:19).

~ MARGARET CLARKSON ~

'O Joy, that seekest me through pain…'

The hymn 'O Love, that wilt not let me go' was written at a time of deep anguish. The author, George Matheson (1842-1906), had lost his sight by the age of eighteen. This was a double tragedy, as his fiancée broke off their engagement when she found out that he would never see again. Many years later, when he was forty, he suffered another loss when the sister who had devoted herself to caring for him left to get married. He wrote: 'I was at that time alone, it was the day of my sister's marriage… Something happened to me, which was known only to myself, and which caused me the most severe mental suffering. The hymn was the fruit of that suffering…. I had the impression of having it dictated to me by some inward voice rather than of working it out myself.' These beautiful lines came to him in about five minutes. Later he changed 'I climb the rainbow' to 'I trace the rainbow' — but that was his only alteration. The central truth of the hymn, that God is with us in grief and pain, is also reflected in this prayer of George Matheson:

Dear God, I have never thanked you for my thorns. I have thanked you a thousand times for my roses but never once for my thorns. Teach me the glory of the cross I bear, teach me the value of my thorns.

O Love, that wilt not let me go,
　I rest my weary soul in thee;
I give thee back the life I owe,
　That in thine ocean depths its flow
　May richer, fuller be.

O Light, that followest all my way,
　I yield my flickering torch to thee;
My heart restores its borrowed ray,
　That in thy sunshine's blaze its day
　May brighter, fairer be.

O Joy, that seekest me through pain,
　I cannot close my heart to thee;
I climb the rainbow through the rain,
　And feel the promise is not vain
　That morn shall tearless be.

O Cross, that liftest up my head,
　I dare not ask to fly from thee;
I lay in dust life's glory dead,
　And from the ground there blossoms red
　Life that shall endless be.

~ GEORGE MATHESON ~

'Set me free from my prison...'

Psalm 142 was composed by David while he was trapped by Saul and in fear of his life. His urgent cry for help expresses the feelings of loneliness and desperation felt by those who are suffering. 'Set me free from my prison' (verse 7) is an apt metaphor for feeling utterly helpless.

> I CRY ALOUD to the LORD;
>   I lift up my voice to the LORD for mercy.
> I pour out my complaint before him;
>   before him I tell my trouble.
>
> When my spirit grows faint within me,
>   it is you who know my way.
>
> Set me free from my prison,
>   that I may praise your name.

~ PSALM 142:1-3,7 ~

Suffering and glory

I CONSIDER that our present sufferings are not worth comparing with the glory that will be revealed in us. The creation waits in eager expectation for the sons of God to be revealed. For the creation was subjected to frustration, not by its own choice, but by the will of the one who subjected it, in hope that the creation itself will be liberated from its bondage to decay and brought into the glorious freedom of the children of God. We know that the whole creation has been groaning as in the pains of childbirth right up to the present time. Not only so, but we ourselves, who have the first fruits of the Spirit, groan inwardly as we wait eagerly for our adoption as sons, the redemption of our bodies.

~ ROMANS 8:18-23 ~

Outwardly wasting away — inwardly being renewed

THEREFORE we do not lose heart. Though outwardly we are wasting away, yet inwardly we are being renewed day by day. For our light and momentary troubles are achieving for us an eternal glory that far outweighs them all. So we fix our eyes not on what is seen, but on what is unseen. For what is seen is temporary, but what is unseen is eternal. Now we know that if the earthly tent we live in is destroyed, we have a building from God, an eternal house in heaven, not built by human hands.

~ 2 CORINTHIANS 4:16 – 5:1 ~

God's providence in all things

AND WE KNOW that in all things God works for the good of those who love him, who have been called according to his purpose. For those God foreknew he also predestined to be conformed to the likeness of his Son, that he might be the firstborn among many brothers. And those he predestined, he also called; those he called, he also justified; those he justified, he also glorified.

What, then, shall we say in response to this? If God is for us, who can be against us? He who did not spare his own Son, but gave him up for us all – how will he not also, along with him, graciously give us all things? Who will bring any charge against those whom God has chosen? It is God who justifies. Who is he that condemns? Christ Jesus, who died – more than that, who was raised to life – is at the right hand of God and is also interceding for us. Who shall separate us from the love of Christ? Shall trouble or hardship or persecution or famine or nakedness or danger or sword? As it is written: 'For your sake we face death all day long; we are considered as sheep to be slaughtered.' No, in all these things we are more than conquerors through him who loved us. For I am convinced that neither death nor life, neither angels nor demons, neither the present nor the future, nor any powers, neither height nor depth, nor anything else in all creation, will be able to separate us from the love of God that is in Christ Jesus our Lord.

~ ROMANS 8:28-39 ~

Sleeplessness

ONE OF THE GREATEST difficulties with which most sufferers have to contend is an inability to sleep. While the rest of the world welcomes the onset of night as happy respite from the burdens of the day and sinks effortlessly into deep and refreshing slumber, most sufferers watch the gathering shadows deepen with apprehension; for trying as the day may have been, the night brings heavier trials. Sleep is evasive, fitful, often impossible; energy ebbs; pain intensifies; fears seem more cogent, worries more pressing... Ours seem to be the words of Job: 'Nights of misery have been assigned to me... The night drags on and I toss till dawn' (JOB 7:3-4).

The writer of PSALM 77 had such a problem: 'At night I stretched out untiring hands and my soul refused to be comforted... You kept my eyes from closing; I was too troubled to speak' (PSALM 77:2,4). But weary and discouraged as he was, the sleepless psalmist, probably by an act of sheer will-power, determined to press beyond his afflictions on to the contemplation of his God. His outlook changed. He was able to analyse his difficulty and to see past it to its solution: 'Then I thought: "To this I will appeal: the years of the right hand of the Most High. I will remember the deeds of the Lord"' (PSALM 77:10-11). And throughout the remainder of PSALM 77, and through all of the next six psalms, the psalmist goes on to recount God's mercies and to sing his praise.

There is no doubt that those who must face continual sleeplessness or restless, fitful sleep, have a very real problem, a true infirmity. Only those who have been confronted with it can know how inexpressibly wearing and devitalizing it is; how it saps away the very energy which is the physical basis of our ability to trust in God and to stay our hearts upon him; how it seeks to erode the very roots of our faith. Yet God, who has said that he knows our down-sittings and uprisings, who is acquainted with all our ways, has not left these sufferers without a way of escape (PSALM 139:1-3).

Doctors tell us that although we may not be able to sleep, it is possible for us to rest; and this is something that every sleepless person must learn to do. What better way can there be than to rest in the Lord and wait patiently for him?

Even if we have lost all sense of his closeness, our unsleeping, unchanging, sovereign, covenant-keeping God is watching with us and over us. He himself passed through a night of darkness deeper than anything we can ever imagine, let alone be called upon to experience; and because for our sakes he was forsaken of the Father, we shall never be forsaken. His is the faithfulness in which we trust, his the strength by which we live, his the grace by which we can be strengthened to endure; and that unfailing source of supply depends not upon our poor, human frailty, nor our ability to feel his presence with us, but on the eternal God himself.

We must rest upon him, be still before him, even claim something of his song, whether we have any conscious-ness of his nearness or not. Even when beset by the ter-ror of night, we stake our all upon his promise and throw our whole weight, body and soul, upon our Saviour; and we find him faithful. 'Weeping may endure for a night, but joy cometh in the morning' (PSALM 30:5).

~ MARGARET CLARKSON ~

A patient heart

Frances Ridley Havergal (1836-1879) wrote a large number of popular hymns (including 'Take my Life', 'Like a river glorious', and 'I am trusting Thee, Lord Jesus'). She knew what it was to suffer severe illness and intense pain, and she died at the early age of forty-two. She asked that her favourite text be inscribed on her tomb: 'The blood of Christ, His Son, cleanseth us from all sin.'

For three or four weeks I was too prostrate for any consecutive prayer, or for even a text to be given me; and this was the time for realizing what 'silent in love' meant (Zephaniah 3:17). And then it seemed doubly sweet when I was again able to 'hold converse' with him. He seemed, too, so often to send answers from his own Word with wonderful power. One evening (after a relapse) I longed so much to be able to pray, but found I was too weak for the least effort of thought, and I only looked up and said, 'Lord Jesus, I am so tired!' And then he brought to my mind 'rest in the Lord', with its lovely marginal reading, 'be *silent* to the Lord', and so I just was silent to him, and he seemed to overflow me with perfect peace, in the sense of his own perfect love. It was worth anything to lie and think that it might be really the Master's home call; but I do think it was worth almost more to find, when the tide turned, that he had really *taken* the will I had laid at his feet, and could and did take away all the disappointment which I had fancied must be so keen at being turned back from the golden gates. I was more astonished

at finding that he could make me quite as glad and willing to live and suffer, as to go straight away to heaven,
than at anything, I think.

> I am not eager, bold, or strong,
>   All that is past;
> I'm ready *not* to do,
>   At last, at last.

> My half-day's work is almost done,
>   'Tis all my part;
> I bring my patient God
>   A patient heart.

For I am quite satisfied to do *half-day*'s work hence-
forth, if he pleases; and well I may be when I have plenty
of proof that he can make a *half-hour*'s work worth a whole
day's if he will: yes, or half-a-minute's either!

Trust Jesus in and for everything. When a trial is past,
one does so bitterly regret not having trusted him entirely
in it; and one sees that we might as well have had all the
joy and rest of perfect trust all along.

~ FRANCES RIDLEY HAVERGAL ~

Illness and our spiritual life

Isobel Kuhn served as a missionary with her husband in China from 1929 to 1950, and in Thailand from 1951 to 1954. She is best known for her many inspirational books, including By Searching. *At the peak of her usefulness she was diagnosed with cancer, and she died at the age of fifty-five. These are some of her reflections on her final illness.*

THERE IS A VALLEY of deep shadows between the place where I live and that to which I shall journey in a very short time. I cannot reach my home in that city of gold without passing through this dark valley of shadows. But I am not afraid, because the best Friend I ever had went through the same valley, long, long ago and drove away all its gloom. *He* has stuck by me through thick and thin since we first became acquainted fifty-five years ago, and I hold his promise in printed form never to forsake me. *He* will be with me as I walk through the valley of shadows, and I shall not lose my way when he is with me… But I have learned this, that the spiritual is tied down to the physical more than is apparent. After my first operation, finding I would have long hours just lying in bed, I said to myself, 'Good. Now I will employ this time in intercession and prayer.' But to my surprise and alarm I found I could not! What was wrong with me? Was I backsliding? Then I realized it. To pray for others as I was accustomed to do required *physical* as well as spiritual strength. … I had no physical strength with which to rally my forces. I just had to lie there and say, 'Well, Lord, I will have to ask you to read my heart as you read the names on the breast-plate of the high priest in days of old.' ... This explains why some of the saints have seemed to find the valley of the shadows a dark place. The Lord is most certainly there with them, but the unconscious habitual use of physical strength in laying hold of this fact by faith may disconcert by its absence...

I have been reading the diary of David Brainerd these days, and have noticed the relation between his own physical well-being or illness and his sense of God's presence. They were often related. When ill in body he bemoaned his spiritual barrenness. 'November 1. Was very much disordered in body and sometimes full of pain.... Alas! When God is withdrawn, all is gone.' Then a few days later after he was rested a bit, he writes: 'Saw more of the glory and majesty of God than ever I had seen before. Oh, how my soul then rejoiced in God!' The spirit is not absolutely dependent on physical well-being ... but it is more closely related than we are sometimes apt to allow.

~ ISOBEL KUHN ~

Aging

The blessings in growing older

EVEN TO YOUR old age and grey hairs I am he, I am he who will sustain you. I have made you and I will carry you; I will sustain you and I will rescue you.

~ ISAIAH 46:4 ~

GREY HAIR is a crown of splendour; it is attained by a righteous life.

~ PROVERBS 16:31 ~

THE RIGHTEOUS will flourish like a palm tree, they will grow like a cedar of Lebanon; planted in the house of the LORD, they will flourish in the courts of our God. They will still bear fruit in old age, they will stay fresh and green, proclaiming, 'The LORD is upright; he is my Rock, and there is no wickedness in him.'

~ PSALM 92:12-15 ~

God's faithfulness throughout life

In you, O Lord, I have taken refuge;
    let me never be put to shame.
Rescue me and deliver me in your righteousness;
    turn your ear to me and save me.
Be my rock of refuge,
    to which I can always go;
give the command to save me,
    for you are my rock and my fortress.
Deliver me, O my God, from the hand of the wicked,
    from the grasp of evil and cruel men.

For you have been my hope, O Sovereign Lord,
    my confidence since my youth.
From my birth I have relied on you;
    you brought me forth from my mother's womb.
    I will ever praise you.
I have become like a portent to many,
    but you are my strong refuge.
My mouth is filled with your praise,
    declaring your splendour all day long.

Do not cast me away when I am old;
  do not forsake me when my strength is gone.

Since my youth, O God, you have taught me,
  and to this day I declare your marvellous deeds.
Even when I am old and grey,
  do not forsake me, O God,
till I declare your power to the next generation,
  your might to all who are to come.

~ PSALM 71:1-9,17-18 ~

The golden bowl is broken

REMEMBER NOW thy Creator in the days of thy youth, while the evil days come not, nor the years draw nigh, when thou shalt say, I have no pleasure in them; While the sun, or the light, or the moon, or the stars, be not darkened, nor the clouds return after the rain: In the day when the keepers of the house shall tremble, and the strong men shall bow themselves, and the grinders cease because they are few, and those that look out of the windows be darkened, And the doors shall be shut in the streets, when the sound of the grinding is low, and he shall rise up at the voice of the bird, and all the daughters of musick shall be brought low; Also when they shall be afraid of that which is high, and fears shall be in the way, and the almond tree shall flourish, and the grasshopper shall be a burden, and desire shall fail: because man goeth to his long home, and the mourners go about the streets: Or ever the silver cord be loosed, or the golden bowl be broken, or the pitcher be broken at the fountain, or the wheel broken at the cistern. Then shall the dust return to the earth as it was: and the spirit shall return unto God who gave it.

~ ECCLESIASTES 12:1-7, KJV ~

Loneliness — and the unchanging friend

Though my father and mother forsake me, the LORD will receive me.

~ PSALM 27:10 ~

LONELINESS CAN BE very real in old age. Some friends prove false; others grow frail and die. Death breaks our closest and dearest relationships. But Jesus Christ is the same yesterday, today and for ever. He is the friend that 'sticks closer than a brother' (PROVERBS 18:24). Nothing can separate us from his love. He will never leave you, and never forsake you (HEBREWS 13:5). Distance may separate us from loved ones. But when Christ ascended to heaven, he promised that the Holy Spirit would come and be with each of his people for ever. As family and friends are taken from us, let us remind ourselves more and more of our mighty and faithful friend. 'Cast all your cares upon him, for he cares for you' (1 PETER 5:7). And if, while we cannot see him, we can still rejoice in him with joy unspeakable and full of glory, how much greater will our joy be when we see him face to face!

~ ANONYMOUS ~

Exceeding great and precious promises

The hymn 'How firm a foundation' was published in 1787 under the title 'Exceeding great and precious promises'. We know nothing about the author. The verses are based on the promises of Scripture. Verse 1 alludes to Hebrews 6:18. Verse 3 almost repeats Isaiah 41:10. Verses 4 and 6 are a paraphrase of Isaiah 43:2. Verse 5 echoes Isaiah 46:4 and Isaiah 40:11. The final verse is based on Hebrews 13:5: 'Never will I leave you; never will I forsake you.'

How FIRM a foundation, ye saints of the Lord,
  Is laid for your faith in his excellent Word!
What more can he say than to you he has said —
  You, who unto Jesus for refuge have fled?

In every condition — in sickness, in health,
  In poverty's vale, or abounding in wealth;
At home or abroad, on the land, on the sea,
  As days may demand, shall thy strength ever be.

Fear not, I am with thee, O be not dismayed!
  I, I am thy God, and will still give thee aid:
I'll strengthen thee, help thee, and cause thee to stand,
  Upheld by my righteous, omnipotent hand.

When through the deep waters I cause thee to go,
　The rivers of woe shall not thee overflow;
For I will be with thee, thy troubles to bless,
　And sanctify to thee thy deepest distress.

E'en down to old age all my people shall prove
　My sovereign, eternal, unchangeable love;
And when silver hairs shall their temples adorn,
　Like lambs they shall still in my bosom be borne.

When through fiery trials thy pathway shall lie,
　My grace all-sufficient shall be thy supply;
The flame shall not hurt thee: I only design
　Thy dross to consume, and thy gold to refine.

The soul that on Jesus has leaned for repose
　I will not, I will not desert to its foes;
That soul, though all hell should endeavour to shake,
　I'll never, no never, no never forsake!

~ 'K' IN RIPPON'S SELECTION 1787 ~

The triumph of faith

William Romaine (1714-1795) was a gifted scholar who was converted after *becoming a Church of England clergyman. He then became a leading revivalist preacher who attracted great crowds, including many extremely poor people. One of his most influential works was* The Triumph of Faith, *in which this essay on old age is found.*

IT IS APPOINTED unto men once to die. The time is fixed by an immutable decree. The length of our days is seventy years, or eighty if we have the strength, yet their span is but trouble and sorrow, for they quickly pass and we fly away (PSALM 90:10). If some are allowed to live longer, then the sickness of old age must arrive, and with it sorrow: both the forerunners of death. Circulation slows down. The senses grow dull. The faculties of the mind may be impaired. Memory may fail.

In this decline of life, Christians suffer the same weaknesses as others. We are not exempt from pain, sickness, or death. But we do have the consolations of God to help us remain patient and joyful. Such consolations are more needed than ever before. He has promised them, and he never fails those who trust him. His promises are exactly suited to the weaknesses of old age which he has described with an unerring pen (ECCLESIASTES 12). He understands our minds and bodies. When we feel the signs of old age, these things are warning signals, showing us that our vigour is declining, and our body is returning to the earth.

It is happy for us if we remember our Creator in the days of our youth, before these wearisome days of weakness and pain arrive. We then prepare for old age by knowing what Jesus has promised to do for his people when heart and flesh begin to fail. We know that the Lord is our helper, and we need not fear what age can do to us.

Abraham, the friend of God, lived to be 175 years old. He died, 'at a good old age, an old man and full of years; and he was gathered to his people' (GENESIS 25:8). He was happy in his last years, for he spent them in faith. When they came to an end he died in peace. With his last breath he committed his spirit into the hands of him who had redeemed it. The Hebrew uses a lovely word here: he was 'satisfied'. The same word is found in PSALM 17:15: "And I – in righteousness I shall see your face; when I awake, I shall be satisfied with seeing your likeness." Abraham was satisfied with what he had enjoyed of the favour and friendship of his God. All the children of Abraham, treading in the steps of his faith, have the same God to deal with, who keeps his covenant for ever.

Isaac also lived to a great age. He experienced many trials, but at 180 years of age he died, satisfied with life, and happy in the prospect beyond death. His son Jacob was 147 years old, when he died. At the end, he declared that he had waited for the salvation of God. Waiting faith is strong faith. After he had blessed his children, and had given directions concerning his bones, Jacob quietly gathered up his feet into the bed as if he had been going to sleep and died in peace.

All these lived in the world, strangers and pilgrims, looking for a city that has foundations, whose Builder and Maker is God (HEBREWS 11:10). Their hope was not disappointed. They died believing. When they came to the end of their lives they came to heaven. The moment they expired they entered the city which God had prepared for them. Their bodies, sleeping in the dust shall be raised and glorified in the morning of the resurrection.

If we reach old age, we are to trust in the God of Abraham, Isaac, and Jacob. Whatever he was to them, he is the same to us – our God as well as theirs. He is our covenant God. He is engaged to glorify both our body and our soul. We are commanded to cast *all* our cares and concerns in extreme old age onto him.

If nature fails, grace cannot. The life of sense may be dying, but the life of faith cannot die. The branches thrive and bring forth fruit in their old age, not of themselves, but because they are grafted into the heavenly vine, in which they live for ever. 'I am the vine', says Jesus, 'you are the branches. If a man abides in me and I in him, he will bear much fruit; apart from me you can do nothing' (JOHN 15:5). He will so fill you with the fruits of righteousness that your last days will be your best days.

Old age is a favourable time for exercising and improving faith. Our activities may be limited, but many things are removed which may have hindered our spiritual lives. Now is the time to learn to walk by faith, and not by sense. Young believers are often tempted to judge themselves by their feelings. Age itself is a sort of deliverance from this temptation. The strength of our body is decaying. The high spirits of youth are abating. Faith grows and flourishes as there is less dependence on other things. As age itself tends to weaken this dependence, it becomes, in the hand of the Holy Spirit, a favourable time to live less upon the things which are seen, and more upon the things which are not seen. Less of sense, more of faith.

But it must be remembered that old age does not automatically produce greater godliness. It is only by God's grace that physical weakness leads to spiritual growth. A non-Christian may use reason and philosophy to try to keep positive, but will probably complain when old age leads to weakness and pains. He may become peevish and fretful. If he is not a friend of God, he cannot look up for divine support when all human support begins to fail. The pressure of severe illness and pain may drive him to impatience and bad temper. Now a Christian in the same circumstances can and should respond differently! His body feels pain, but his mind can be comfortable and at ease. God can give patience to bear his sufferings, and grace to profit from them. Yes, the peace of God rules in his heart. An elderly person with the peace of God ruling in his heart will have a thankful spirit: the infallible antidote against all the challenges of old age.

~ WILLIAM ROMAINE ~

Prayer of an elderly Christian: 'You are taking down my earthly tent with much tenderness and love'

IT IS TRUE, my body is very ill, but, thank you Lord for my sound mind. Age has brought upon me great weakness, but this makes more room for your power. I have many pains, but you, Lord, have more comforts. In the worst of pain, you keep me patient. 'Father, your will be done.' I have an afflicted body, but I have a happy heart. My encouragements are great, your consolations many. I feel the symptoms of old age warning me daily of my approaching death. Through grace I take the warning. They find me living, and I hope they will find me dying, in the faith of the Son of God.

You are taking down my earthly 'tent' with much tenderness and love. You have prepared a house not made with hands, eternal in the heavens. May you never leave me nor forsake me, 'til I be with you, where you are, and be like Christ and enjoy him for ever and ever! Yet a very, very little while – hold on, faith and patience – and I shall see Jesus in his glory, which is the heaven of heavens.

Lord Jesus Christ, my merciful and faithful High Priest, thank you for your kind promises to the elderly and ill. You have exactly fitted these promises to our weaknesses. You are with us always to help in time of need. I begin to feel great weakness, even approaching death. I look to you, almighty Jesus, for your promised grace. Grant me constant supplies of your Spirit. May my illness and weakness force me to stay close to you. May I be kept humble. May I pray more. Keep me thankful. Your arm is not shortened. Your compassions never fail. Stand by me then, and hold me up according to thy word. Make me strong in thy strength, that I may daily put more honour upon thy love and thy power.

In the decline of life let me never doubt your faithfulness to support and comfort me. Grant me the consolations of God. When my heart and flesh fail, then be the strength of my heart and my portion for ever. When I am weak in myself, then make me strong in you. If it be your holy will that I should become quite helpless, make me to lie quiet in your hand, believing that you are my salvation. Grant me this, Lord Jesus; for your mercy's sake, let me die in faith. Amen.

~ WILLIAM ROMAINE ~

'Abide with me'

Henry F. Lyte (1793-1847) had a godly mother, but his father abandoned the family when he was a small boy. At the age of nine, his mother died. A kind minister and his wife cared for Henry. He was ordained in 1815 and spent much of his ministry in Brixham, Devon. His health broke down due to overwork, and he preached his final sermon at the age of fifty-four: 'I stand here among you today, as alive from the dead. I hope to induce you to prepare for that solemn hour which must come to all.' Shortly before his death, he penned 'Abide with me'.

In these verses, Lyte expressed a prayer that his writing would be spiritually useful:

> But might I leave behind
> Some blessing for my fellows, some fair trust
> To guide, to cheer, to elevate my kind,
> When I am in the dust.
>
> O thou, whose touch can lend
> Life to the dead, thy quickening grace supply,
> And grant me, swanlike, my last breath to spend
> In song that may not die!

The abiding popularity of 'Abide with me' suggests that Lyte's prayer was answered.

ABIDE WITH ME; fast falls the eventide;
  The darkness deepens; Lord with me abide.
When other helpers fail and comforts flee,
  Help of the helpless, O abide with me.

Swift to its close ebbs out life's little day;
  Earth's joys grow dim; its glories pass away;
Change and decay in all around I see;
  O thou who changest not, abide with me.

Not a brief glance I beg, a passing word;
  But as thou dwell'st with thy disciples,
Lord, familiar, condescending, patient, free.
  Come not to sojourn, but abide with me.

Come not in terrors, as the King of kings,
  But kind and good, with healing in thy wings,
Tears for all woes, a heart for every plea —
  Come, Friend of sinners, and thus abide with me.

Thou on my head in early youth didst smile;
  And, though rebellious and perverse meanwhile,
Thou hast not left me, oft as I left thee,
  On to the close, O Lord, abide with me.

I need thy presence every passing hour.
  What but thy grace can foil the tempter's power?
Who, like thyself, my guide and stay can be?
  Through cloud and sunshine, Lord, abide with me.

...continued

I fear no foe, with thee at hand to bless;
  Ills have no weight, and tears no bitterness.
Where is death's sting? Where, grave, thy victory?
  I triumph still, if thou abide with me.

Hold thou thy cross before my closing eyes;
  Shine through the gloom and point me to the skies.
Heaven's morning breaks, and earth's vain shadows flee;
  In life, in death, O Lord, abide with me.

~ HENRY F. LYTE ~

The loss of memory

HOW UNRELIABLE our memory becomes as we get older!
We forget so many everyday details, and sometimes the
events of the past seem almost like a dream. The memory
of old friends becomes uncertain, we may even forget their
names. Sometimes an extremely elderly person possesses a
perfect memory, but more often as the years go by we
find our memory becoming less and less sharp. We should
not be either surprised or impatient when this happens: it
is a reminder of our mortality.

This present world will not be our home forever,
though we often live as if it will be. When our minds and
bodies grow weaker, it is a reminder that we are reaching
the evening of life, and we are to get ready for the dawn
of immortality. But this very weakness also means that we
have to step back from some of the business of life. We
may well find that we have more time for thought –
which means we are able to prepare for eternity. We may
also find that we are afflicted with more sickness and
pain, which means that we may be more willing to think
of leaving this present life and entering the next.

This is not to minimize the distress caused by the failure
of memory. One friend in her seventieth year wrote
despondently: 'My memory gets worse every day. I can't
remember where I put anything, even for one hour. I
could have a place for everything: but I forget that I forget! You can't imagine how upsetting this is unless you've
experienced it. It is just as bad when it comes to appoint-
ments and dates. I have to make a note of everything, and

then I lose the note! However, I have to remember that Jesus is my guarantee that all will be well in the end. He never forgets! All my concerns are in his hands.'

In the confusion of a failing memory, take comfort in this knowledge that God never forgets you! He still takes an interest in your smallest concerns.

> Can a mother forget the baby at her breast and have no compassion on the child she has borne? Though she may forget, I will not forget you! See I have engraved you on the palms of my hands (ISAIAH 49:15-16).

So God will not forget you. But take comfort also from the fact that even when elderly Christians forget everything else, the name of Jesus often remains unspeakably precious to them. When Bishop Beveridge was dying, he was unable to recognize any of his relatives, his friends, or even his own wife. But when someone asked, 'Do you know the Lord Jesus Christ?' he replied without any hesitation: 'Jesus Christ! oh, yes, I have known him these forty years! He is my only hope.'

When we reach heaven, we shall no longer have to complain of the imperfection of memory. Then we shall remember every detail of how God has led us so faithfully and lovingly for so many years. How wonderful that will that be! The light of eternity will shine on the records of the past. Every page of our life will be clear and legible. We shall read the pages without pain or regret. At the moment, remembering the past is often tinged with regret. It will not be so in heaven! We will have a perfectly clear memory of our life from birth to death, and yet our understanding of God's providence will be so deep, and we will be so submitted to his wise and perfect will, that there will be no cause for grief. Rather, we will have so many proofs of God's tenderness and care that we will be filled with gratitude and praise. Then, as we recall with accurate minuteness the circumstances of our earthly history, we shall see enough of God's marvellous wisdom and loving-kindness to excite our praise throughout all eternity.

So rather than bemoaning our present loss, let us look forward to the future! Everyday we are closer to the new heavens and the new earth. There we will enjoy mental and physical energy for ever. For now, our weakened intellect, declining strength, and failing memory are tokens that it will not be very long before we are at rest.

Let us look forward! When we consider the wonder of heaven, let us not spend too much time complaining that we can no longer enjoy the things of earth. It may feel as though a mist is gathering over the scenes of earth, but everlasting sunshine is about to break forth.

~ ANONYMOUS ~

My journey into Alzheimer's disease

Robert Davis was a well-loved minister of a large Presbyterian church in Miami. At the early age of fifty-three he was diagnosed with Alzheimer's disease, and had to resign from the ministry. As his condition worsened, with the help of his wife Betty he made a record of what it felt like.

I CAN NO LONGER remember a list that goes above five items. I sometimes become confused and lost even in familiar stores. I can no longer read even such simple things as long magazine articles. I can become lost in a motel room and not even be able to find the door to the bathroom. All mathematical skills are gone. My mind has become a sieve that can only catch and hold certain random things. My IQ has dropped in half.

I could not even remember what my mother looked like, nor could I picture even the fondest of our family memories that I so cherished. Again, in the privacy of my hospital room, I cried about this loss...

Gradually, because of not hearing, not remembering, or not comprehending, fear swept over me as I lost more and more control of my circumstances. I was gripped by paranoia. The saddest part is that I became distrustful of those who loved me and had my best interest at heart.

I saw what was happening in me and I could name it at the time as paranoia. However, even though I saw it happening to me, I could do nothing to stop the feelings.

This paranoia that accompanies Alzheimer's makes me fearful of so many things and has completely changed my personality.

Perhaps the first spiritual change I noticed was fear. I have never really known fear before. At night when it is total blackness, these absurd fears come. The comforting memories can't be reached. The mind-sustaining Bible verses are gone. The old emotions are gone as new, uncontrolled, fearful emotions sweep in to replace them. The sweetness of prayer and the gentle comfort of the Holy Spirit are gone.

Sometimes these fears come even in the daylight as I am gripped in a trance-like state. In such a condition, people can even talk to me and I can grunt a response while those speaking to me have no idea what is happening inside me.

When I realize these fears are coming on, I have found that I have to physically move to break the spell. Often it is not enough to just move a part of my body, but I have to make my whole body move. I take a brisk shower, ride my exercise bike, or go for a walk. After such stimulation, the spell is broken, and I am saved from this internal torment. Since this works so well for me, I have to wonder if the ceaseless walking and wandering of Alzheimer's patients is their effort to raise themselves out of this agony of their own fears.

Neither prayer, nor Bible reading, nor meditation, nor assurances from friends, nor Christian radio, television, or tape programs bring any comfort in such a state. This is an organic physiological problem produced by the malfunctioning of the brain.

There is a way to help in these terror-filled times, but

it is definitely not by reasoning with the patient. This is the time for comfort, reassurance, a soft touch, and a gentle voice with soothing words or even songs, if you are so gifted. Whatever body language speaks peace in your family can be put to good use in this situation. As soon as my wife is aware that I am in one of these states, she embraces me and strokes me. She asks me to tell her about what was bothering me. As I talk about it, the panic subsides and I am made aware that I am in touch with reality again and that I am once more saved from the black hole.

Over the years I have had to deal with dear, aged Christians with one form or another of dementia who have gone through such spiritual despair. I wish I had known how penetratingly they felt this internal blackness. I remember trying to shock them back to faith by rolling out a barrage of Bible verses and demanding if they still believed this. How I wish I could go back to these dear old friends! Now I would put my arms around them, love them, tell them again the old story of Jesus, our good and faithful Saviour and Shepherd. I would hold their hand and assure them anew as I prayed with them. How much strength I could have given them by reaching out and holding them! Now I more fully realize why we see the word 'touch' associated with Jesus so many times in the Gospels.

My glimmer of hope comes as I realize that these glorious words of that old hymn, 'The love of God', were found written on the wall of a mental hospital.

> Could we with ink the ocean fill,
>   And were the skies of parchment made,

Were every stalk on earth a quill,
 And every man a scribe by trade,
To write the love of God above
 Would drain the ocean dry.
 Nor could the scroll contain the whole,
 Though stretched from sky to sky.

Perhaps the journey that takes me away from reality into the blackness of that place of the blank, emotionless, unmoving Alzheimer's stare is in reality a journey into the richest depths of God's love that few have experienced on earth. Who can know what goes on deep inside a person who is so withdrawn? At that time, I will be unable to give you a clue, but perhaps we can talk about it later in the timeless joy of heaven.

~ ROBERT DAVIS ~

'Our God, our help in ages past'

Isaac Watts (1674-1748) is considered the father of English hymnody. At the time of his birth, his father was in prison for refusing to conform to the State Church. In his turn, Isaac, though offered scholarships to study at University, declined them as this would have committed him to ministering in the Anglican Church. (At that time, Dissenters were not allowed to study at University). Instead, he attended a leading Nonconformist academy, and became an Independent minister in London. Despite continual ill-health, he wrote nearly thirty theological works, and a logic textbook that was used at Harvard, Yale, Oxford and Cambridge. But his greatest contribution to the church lay in his hymns: 697 of them. 'Our God, our help in ages past' is one of the best loved; it is based on Psalm 90:1-5.

OUR GOD, our help in ages past,
　Our hope for years to come,
Our shelter from the stormy blast,
　And our eternal home.

Under the shadow of thy throne
　Thy saints have dwelt secure;
Sufficient is thine arm alone,
　And our defence is sure.

Before the hills in order stood,
　Or earth received her frame,
From everlasting thou art God,
　To endless years the same.

Thy word commands our flesh to dust,
   'Return, ye sons of men':
All nations rose from earth at first,
   And turn to earth again.

A thousand ages, in thy sight,
   Are like an evening gone;
Short as the watch that ends the night
   Before the rising sun.

The busy tribes of flesh and blood,
   With all their lives and cares,
Are carried downwards by the flood,
   And lost in following years.

Time, like an ever-rolling stream,
   Bears all its sons away;
They fly, forgotten, as a dream
   Dies at the opening day.

Like flowery fields the nations stand
   Pleased with the morning light;
The flowers, beneath the mower's hand,
   Lie withering, ere 'tis night.

Our God, our help in ages past,
   Our hope for years to come,
Be thou our guard while troubles last,
   And our eternal home.

~ ISAAC WATTS ~

My resting place

Horatius Bonar (1808-1889) wrote over 600 hymns, and was known as the 'Prince of Scottish hymn-writers'. He was one of eleven children; his younger brother was Andrew Bonar, also a minister. Horatius, Andrew, Robert M'Cheyne and William Burns were among the ministers involved in a powerful revival in Scotland during the 1830s and 1840s. Horatius and his wife Jane suffered the heartbreak of seeing five of their young children die in succession. Later, one of his grown daughters was widowed and came to live with her parents, bringing her five young children with her. Horatius said: 'God took five children from life some years ago, and he has given me another five to bring up for him in my old age.'

His best-loved hymns, such as 'Thy works, not mine, O Christ', and 'Not what these hands have done' have the theme of the exaltation of Christ, and our unworthiness.

I HEARD the voice of Jesus say,
  'Come unto Me and rest;
Lay down, thou weary one, lay down
  thy head upon My breast.'
I came to Jesus as I was,
  weary and worn and sad;
I found in him a resting place,
  and he has made me glad.

I heard the voice of Jesus say,
  'Behold, I freely give
The living water; thirsty one,
  stoop down, and drink, and live.'
I came to Jesus, and I drank
  of that life giving stream;
My thirst was quenched, my soul revived,
  and now I live in him.

I heard the voice of Jesus say,
  'I am this dark world's Light;
Look unto Me, thy morn shall rise,
  and all thy day be bright.'
I looked to Jesus, and I found
  in him my Star, my Sun;
And in that light of life I'll walk,
  till travelling days are done.

~ HORATIUS BONAR ~

Becoming more like Christ

As WE ADVANCE in life we should be more considerate, more kind, more like Christ, not less so; and if we abide in him and his words abide in us, there can be no doubt that we shall grow in grace. The stream of Christian affection will become deeper, not shallower; the flame of unselfish love will burn more brightly, instead of almost going out.

~ ANONYMOUS ~

FACING *death*

Absent from the body, present with the Lord

WE LIVE BY FAITH, not by sight. We are confident, I say, and would prefer to be away from the body and at home with the Lord.

~ 2 CORINTHIANS 5:7-8 ~

FOR ME to live is Christ and to die is gain. If I am to go on living in the body, this will mean fruitful labour for me. Yet what shall I choose? I do not know! I am torn between the two: I desire to depart and be with Christ which is better by far; but it is more necessary for you that I remain in the body.

~ PHILIPPIANS 1:21-24 ~

THEN I HEARD a voice from heaven say, 'Write: Blessed are the dead who die in the Lord from now on.' 'Yes', says the Spirit, 'they will rest from their labour, for their deeds will follow them.'

~ REVELATION 14:13 ~

In Revelation, the souls of dead believers are shown to be in the immediate presence of God, until Christ's second coming and the judgement.

WHEN HE OPENED the fifth seal, I saw under the altar the souls of those who had been slain because of the word of God and the testimony they had maintained. They called out in a loud voice, 'How long, Sovereign Lord, holy and true, until you judge the inhabitants of earth and avenge our blood?'

~ REVELATION 6:9-10 ~

When one of the criminals crucified along with Jesus repented,

JESUS ANSWERED him, 'I tell you the truth, today you will be with me in paradise.'

~ LUKE 23:43 ~

'Underneath are the everlasting arms'

The great English preacher Charles Haddon Spurgeon preached a magnificent sermon on Deuteronomy 33:27 in 1887, just a few years before his death. He was already suffering considerably through ill health, so the following extract is especially poignant:

THERE ARE TIMES in a person's life when he has to come down. It is not a very easy matter to go down the hill safely. Some persons have proved that it is difficult to grow old gracefully; but to the Christian it ought not to be impossible or unusual. Still, there are difficulties about that coming down the hill of life: coming down in a very material sense, perhaps, from independence to real poverty; coming down as to your mental powers, being conscious of losing your former influence over your peers, coming down in general repute, through no fault of your own, but through circumstances of which you are not the master. All this is very trying to human nature. You know that, on the way to heaven, there are many Hill Difficulties; and brave spirits rather enjoy climbing to the top of them. We like a craggy path, hard and rough, where we can keep on looking upward all the way even if we have to scramble on our hands and knees. There is something pleasant in going up in that fashion; but it is when going down into the Valley of Humiliation that we are apt to slip. We do not like going down; and, as many horses fall at the bottom of the hill, so I believe that many people trip at the end of a trial when they think it is nearly over, and they have no need to look so carefully to their feet. Well now, dear friends, if any of you are going down the hill, I think the text comes in very beautifully: 'Underneath are the everlasting arms.' You cannot go so low but that God's arms of love are lower still. You get poorer, but 'underneath are the everlasting arms'. You get older and weaker; your ears and eyes may fail, 'underneath are the everlasting arms'. By and by, unless the Lord speedily returns, you will have to die, and you will come down very low then; but still it will be true 'underneath are the everlasting arms'. Earthly comforts will fail you; friends will be unable to help you. They cannot go with you on the great voyage upon which you are about to be launched. When heart and flesh fail, then may the Lord himself say to you, 'Underneath are the everlasting arms'!

~ CHARLES HADDON SPURGEON ~

'The Sun of Righteousness... fills the whole hemisphere'

Edward Payson (1783-1827) ministered in Portland, Maine, New England, and saw a number of revivals in his congregation. His sermons and writings were infused with a conscious longing for heaven. At the age of forty-four, he died of tuberculosis. His family had suffered with him as they witnessed the horrible coughing and decline characteristic of that disease. The last weeks of his life were remarkable for the clear foretastes of glory he enjoyed. He wrote the following to his sister shortly before dying:

THE CELESTIAL CITY is full in my view. Its glories beam upon me, its breezes fan me, its odours are wafted to me, its sounds strike upon my ear, and its spirit is breathed into my heart. Nothing separates me from it but the river of death, which now appears as an insignificant trickle that may be crossed at a single step whenever God shall give permission. The Sun of Righteousness has been gradually drawing nearer and nearer, appearing larger and brighter as he approached, and now he fills the whole hemisphere, pouring forth a flood of glory in which I seem to float like an insect in the beams of the sun, exalting yet almost trembling while I gaze on this excessive brightness, and wonder why God should deign thus to shine upon a sinful worm. A single heart and a single tongue seem altogether inadequate to my wants: I want a whole heart for every separate emotion and a whole tongue to express that emotion.

~ EDWARD PAYSON ~

'Yet will I fear no ill'

This paraphrase of Psalm 23 has been a comfort to many in situations of fear and in times of sickness.

THE LORD's my Shepherd, I'll not want.
　He makes me down to lie
In pastures green; he leadeth me
　The quiet waters by.

My soul he doth restore again;
　And me to walk doth make
Within the paths of righteousness,
　Even for his own Name's sake.

Yea, though I walk in death's dark vale,
　Yet will I fear no ill;
For thou art with me; and thy rod
　And staff my comfort still.

My table thou hast furnishèd
　In presence of my foes;
My head thou dost with oil anoint,
　And my cup overflows.

Goodness and mercy all my life
　Shall surely follow me;
And in God's house forevermore
　My dwelling place shall be.

~ SCOTTISH PSALTER, 1650 ~

The prospect of heaven gives courage in the face of death

John Bradford (1510-1555) was imprisoned in 1553 by Queen
Mary, and kept in the Tower of London for eighteen months
before being burned at Smithfield on 1 July 1553. He remained
steadfast to the gospel, even though he knew it would cost him
his life. During those months of imprisonment he reflected much
on heaven, convinced that the pains of death would be but the
entry into the presence of the Lord he loved so much:

> I AM ASSURED that though I want here,
>   I have riches there;
> Though I hunger here, I shall have fullness there;
> Though I faint here, I shall be refreshed there;
> And though I be accounted here as a dead man,
>   I shall there live in perpetual glory.
>
> That is the city promised to the captives
>   whom Christ shall make free;
> That is the kingdom assured to them
>   whom Christ shall crown;
> There is the light that shall never go out;
> There is the health that shall never be impaired;
> There is the glory that shall never be defaced;
> There is the life that shall taste no death;
> And there is the portion
>   that passes all the world's preferment.

There is the world that shall never wax worse;
There is every want supplied
  freely without money;
There is not danger, but happiness,
  and honour, and singing,
  and praise and thanksgiving
  unto the heavenly Jehovah,
To him that sits on the throne,
  to the Lamb that here was led to the slaughter,
  that now reigns:
With whom I shall reign
  after I have run this comfortless race
  through this miserable earthly vale.

~ JOHN BRADFORD ~

'Alone with none but you, my God'

As a missionary to the pagans in Britain, Columba (A.D. 521-597) often braved fierce and hostile enemies — alone. They trusted in their gods, their superstitions and rituals. He trusted in the one true God. This magnificent hymn expresses his belief that he was immortal, until his work was done.

ALONE WITH NONE but you, my God,
   I journey on my way:
what need I fear, when you are near,
   O King of night and day?
More safe am I within your hand,
than if a host did round me stand.

My destined time is fixed by you ;
   and death's appointed hour;
though warriors strong around me throng
   they could not halt its power:
no walls of stone defend us here
when comes your final messenger.

My life I yield to your decree,
    and bow to your control
in peaceful calm, for from your arm
    no power can snatch my soul:
no earthly omens can appal
the one who heeds God's heavenly call.

The child of God need fear no ill,
    his chosen, dread no foe;
we leave our fate with you, and wait
    your bidding when to go:
for not from chance our comfort springs –
you are our trust, O King of kings!

~ ATTRIBUTED TO COLUMBA ~
© PRAISE TRUST

Crossing the river

John Bunyan (1628-1688), a poor tinker, fought in the English Civil War on the Parliamentary side. He was recognized as a preacher by his Independent congregation in Bedford in 1657. Following the Restoration of Charles II in 1660 he spent most of the next twelve years in Bedford prison for the 'crime' of preaching without a license. The Pilgrim's Progress was written during his imprisonment, and published in 1678. Within fifty years, it is said that most homes in England had a copy, and it has been more widely read than any book in English except the Bible.

In the following extract from The Pilgrim's Progress, *at the end of his long and dangerous journey, Christian has the final river to cross before entering the Celestial City:*

Now I FURTHER SAW, that between them and the gate was a river; but there was no bridge to go over. The river was very deep. At the sight, therefore, of this river the pilgrims were much stunned; but the men that went with them said, You must go through, or you cannot come at the gate…

The pilgrims then, especially Christian, began to despond, and looked this way and that, but could find no way by which they might escape the river. Then they asked the men if the waters were all of the same depth. They said, No: yet they could not help them in that case; for, said they, you shall find it deeper or shallower, as you believe in the King of the place.

Then they addressed themselves to the water, and entering, Christian began to sink, and crying out to his good friend Hopeful, he said, I sink in deep waters; the billows go over my head all the waves go over me.

Then said the other, Be of good cheer, my brother; I feel the bottom, and it is good. Then said Christian, Ah! my friend, the sorrows of death have compassed me about; I shall not see the land that floweth with milk and honey. And with that a great darkness and horror fell upon Christian, so that he could not see before him. Also here he in a great measure lost his senses, so that he could neither remember nor orderly talk of any of those sweet refreshments that he had met with in the way of his pilgrimage. But all the words that he spoke still tended to discover that he had horror of mind, and heart-fears that he should die in that river, and never obtain entrance in at the gate. Here also, as they who stood by perceived, he was much in the troublesome thoughts of the sins that he had committed, both since and before he began to be a pilgrim. It was also observed that he was troubled with apparitions of hobgoblins and evil spirits; for ever and anon he would intimate so much by words.

Hopeful therefore here had much ado to keep his brother's head above water; yea, sometimes he would be quite gone down, and then, ere a while, he would rise up again, half dead. Hopeful also would endeavour to comfort him, saying, Brother, I see the gate, and men standing by to receive us... These troubles and distresses that you go through are no sign that God hath forsaken you; but are sent to try you, whether you will call to mind that which heretofore you have received of his goodness, and live upon him in your distresses.

Then I saw in my dream that Christian was in a muse a while. To whom also Hopeful added these words, Be of good cheer; Jesus Christ maketh thee whole. And with that Christian brake out with a loud voice, Oh, I see him again! and he tells me, 'When thou passest through the waters, I will be with thee; and through the rivers, they shall not overflow thee' (ISAIAH 43:2). Then they both took courage, and the enemy was after that as still as a stone, until they were gone over. Christian therefore presently found ground to stand upon, and so it followed that the rest of the ground was but shallow. Thus they got over.

Now, upon the bank of the river, on the other side, they saw the two Shining Men again, who there waited for them… Thus they went towards the gate… a company of the heavenly host came out to meet them; to whom it was said by the other two Shining Ones, 'These are the men that have loved our Lord when they were in the world, and that have forsaken all for his holy name; and he hath sent us to fetch them, and we have brought them thus far on their desired journey, that they may go in and look their Redeemer in the face with joy.' Then the heavenly host gave a great shout, saying, 'Blessed are they that are called to the marriage supper of the Lamb' (REVELATION 19:9).

Now I saw in my dream that these two men went in at the gate; and, lo! as they entered, they were transfigured, and they had raiment put on that shone like gold. There were also those that met them with harps and crowns, and gave them the harps to praise withal, and the crowns in token of honour. Then I heard in my dream that all the bells in the city rang again for joy, and that it was said unto them, 'Enter ye into the joy of your Lord.' I also heard the men themselves sing with a loud voice, 'Blessing and honour and glory and power be unto him that sitteth upon the throne and unto the

Lamb for ever and ever' (REVELATION 5:13). ...

Now, just as the gates were opened to let in the men, I looked in after them, and, behold, the city shone like the sun: the streets also were paved with gold; and in them walked many men with crowns on their heads, palms in their hands, and golden harps to sing praises withal.

~ JOHN BUNYAN ~

YOU WILL KEEP in perfect peace him whose mind is steadfast, because he trusts in you.

~ ISAIAH 26:3 ~

The Lord will provide

John Newton (1725-1807) lived a godless and dissolute life before his conversion, even working as a slave trader. His wonder at God's goodness to him was expressed in his hymn 'Amazing Grace'. This less known hymn expresses his certainty that God takes care of his people right through life, and through death as well.

THOUGH troubles assail,
   And dangers affright,
Though friends should all fail
   And foes all unite;
Yet one thing secures us,
   However we're tried:
The Scripture assures us,
   The LORD will provide.

When Satan appears
   And hinders our path,
And fills us with fears,
   We triumph by faith;
He cannot take from us,
   Though often has tried,
This heart-cheering promise,
   The LORD will provide.

No strength of our own
  Or goodness we claim;
Yet since we have known
  The Saviour's great name;
In this our strong tower
  For safety we hide,
The LORD is our power,
  The LORD will provide.

When life sinks apace,
  And death is in view,
This word of his grace
  Shall carry us through:
No fearing or doubting
  With CHRIST on our side,
We hope to die shouting,
  The LORD will provide.

~ JOHN NEWTON ~

'Rock of Ages'

Augustus Montague Toplady (1740-1778) was born in Surrey, but went to Dublin to study. He was converted at the age of sixteen. Later in life he wondered at God's grace, bringing him to Christ in a barn, in an obscure rural area of Ireland, through a sermon preached by a man who could hardly spell his name! He became a strong exponent of Calvinist theology. In 1776 he published an article on the doctrines of grace in the Gospel Magazine, *and in the middle of the article he placed this hymn. It contains a wealth of biblical imagery. Moses struck a rock in the wilderness to provide water for God's people; Christ was struck on the Cross, and provides the 'living water' of salvation. Moses was given refuge in a cleft of rock to hide him from the burning holiness of God. As believers shelter in Christ, they are protected from the wrath of God against their sins. A later (undocumented) story said that Toplady composed this hymn while sheltering from a violent storm in Cheddar Gorge.*

Toplady died of consumption at the age of thirty-eight. As he neared death, he said:

'My heart beats every day stronger and stronger for glory. Sickness is no affliction, pain no cause, death itself no dissolution... My prayers are now all converted into praise.'

ROCK OF AGES, cleft for me,
  Let me hide myself in thee;
Let the water and the blood,
  From thy riven side which flowed,
Be of sin the double cure;
  Cleanse me from its guilt and power.

Not the labours of my hands
  Can fulfil thy law's demands;
Could my zeal no respite know,
  Could my tears for ever flow,
All for sin could not atone:
  Thou must save, and thou alone.

Nothing in my hand I bring,
  Simply to thy cross I cling;
Naked, come to thee for dress;
  Helpless, look to thee for grace;
Foul, I to the fountain fly;
  Wash me, Saviour, or I die.

While I draw this fleeting breath,
  When my eyelids close in death,
When I soar through tracts unknown,
  See thee on thy judgement throne;
Rock of Ages, cleft for me,
  Let me hide myself in thee.

~ AUGUSTUS MONTAGUE TOPLADY ~

'We will not fear'

GOD IS OUR refuge and strength,
  an ever-present help in trouble.
Therefore we will not fear,
  though the earth give way
  and the mountains fall into
  the heart of the sea,
though its waters roar and foam
  and the mountains quake with their surging.

There is a river whose streams
  make glad the city of God,
  the holy place where the Most High dwells.

'Be still, and know that I am God;
  I will be exalted among the nations,
  I will be exalted in the earth.'

The LORD Almighty is with us;
  the God of Jacob is our fortress.

~ PSALM 46:1-4,10-11 ~

'Where, O death, is your sting?'

I DECLARE TO YOU, brothers, that flesh and blood cannot inherit the kingdom of God, nor does the perishable inherit the imperishable. Listen, I tell you a mystery: We will not all sleep, but we will all be changed – in a flash, in the twinkling of an eye, at the last trumpet. For the trumpet will sound, the dead will be raised imperishable, and we will be changed. For the perishable must clothe itself with the imperishable, and the mortal with immortality. When the perishable has been clothed with the imperishable, and the mortal with immortality, then the saying that is written will come true: 'Death has been swallowed up in victory.'

'Where, O death, is your victory?
Where, O death, is your sting?'

The sting of death is sin, and the power of sin is the law. But thanks be to God! He gives us the victory through our Lord Jesus Christ.

Therefore, my dear brothers, stand firm. Let nothing move you. Always give yourselves fully to the work of the Lord, because you know that your labour in the Lord is not in vain.

~ I CORINTHIANS 15:50-58 ~

On facing death

Augustine of Hippo (A.D. 354-430), the great apologist for Christianity, wrote:

> WE ARE TO BE SO reduced as to have nothing to present before God but our wretchedness and his mercy. We are so wretched in our sinfulness that nothing else can ever save us except his mercy. But thank God, his mercy is all we need!

> ~ AUGUSTINE ~

Ambrose, Bishop of Milan (circa A.D. 339-397), an early church leader, was asked whether he was not afraid to face God at the judgement. He replied:

> WE HAVE a good Master.

> ~ AMBROSE ~

John Flavel (1630-1691), a Puritan minister and author, wrote:

To BE LIFTED from a bed of sickness to a throne of glory! To leave a sinful troublesome world, a sick and pained body and be in a moment perfectly cured and feel yourself perfectly well and free from all troubles... You cannot imagine what this will be like.

~ JOHN FLAVEL ~

Adoniram Judson (1788-1850), an American missionary to Burma, said near the end of his life:

WHEN CHRIST calls me home, I shall go with the gladness of a boy bounding away from his school.

~ ADONIRAM JUDSON ~

'Just as I am'

Charlotte Elliott (1789-1871) suffered ill health for much of her life. She often felt frustrated at the seeming uselessness of her invalid existence, but from that feeling of inadequacy she was inspired to write one of the great hymns of trust:

> JUST AS I AM, without one plea,
>   But that thy blood was shed for me,
> And that thou bid'st me come to thee,
>   O Lamb of God, I come.
>
> Just as I am, and waiting not
>   To rid my soul of one dark blot,
> To thee whose blood can cleanse each spot,
>   O Lamb of God, I come.
>
> Just as I am, though tossed about
>   With many a conflict, many a doubt,
> Fightings and fears within, without,
>   O Lamb of God, I come.

Just as I am, poor, wretched, blind:
  Sight, riches, healing of the mind,
Yea, all I need in thee to find,
  O Lamb of God, I come.

Just as I am, thou wilt receive,
  Wilt welcome, pardon, cleanse, relieve;
Because thy promise I believe,
  O Lamb of God, I come.

Just as I am – thy love unknown
  Has broken every barrier down –
Now to be thine, yea, thine alone,
  O Lamb of God, I come.

Just as I am, of that free love
  The breadth, length, depth and height to prove,
Here for a season, then above,
  O Lamb of God, I come!

~ CHARLOTTE ELLIOTT ~

I do not fear death

Someone once made a remark to Frances Ridley Havergal about 'death, which we all dread'. Frances responded with this meditation:

No, NOT 'ALL!' One who has seen and accepted God's way of salvation, does not dread death. Perhaps I shall best express myself by doing it very personally — just giving my own experience.

I do not fear death. Often I wake in the night and think of it, look forward to it, with a thrill of joyful expectation and anticipation, which would become impatience, were it not that Jesus is my Master, as well as my Saviour, and I feel I have work to do for him that I would not shirk, and also that *his* time to call me home will be the best and right time; therefore I am content to wait...

It was not always thus. I know as well as any one, what it is to 'dread death', and to put away the thought of its absolute certainty, because I dare not look it in the face. I deserved hell in many ways, but in one most of all, this — that I owed the whole love of my heart to God, and had not given it to him; that Jesus had so loved me as to die for me, and yet I had treated him with daily, hourly ingratitude. I had broken the first commandment, and as I owed all my life — future and past — to God, I had literally 'nothing to pay'; for living to him, and keeping his commands for the future, would not atone for the past. I saw the sinfulness of my heart and life. I could not make my heart better. 'The soul that sins shall die.' So, unless sin is taken away, my soul must die and go to hell.

Where then was my hope? In the same Word of God 'He that believes on the Son has everlasting life: and he that believes not the Son shall not see life; but the wrath of God abides on him' (JOHN 3:36).

I believe what? – that he must keep his word and punish sin, and that he has punished it in the person of Jesus, our Substitute, 'Who his own self bore our sins in his own body on the tree' (1 PETER 2:24).

If Jesus has paid my debt, and borne the punishment of my sins, I simply accept this, and believe him, and it is all a true and real transaction. I did this – I believed it, and cast myself, utterly in hopeless and helpless in myself, at the feet of Jesus, took him at his word, and accepted what he had done for me.

Result? – Joy, peace in believing, and a happy, FULL trust in him, which death cannot touch.

Now it is a reality of realities to me – it is so intertwined with my life, that I know nothing could separate me from his love.

I could not do without Jesus. I cannot and I do not live without him. It is a *new* and different life; and the life and light which takes away all fear of death, is what I want others to have and enjoy.

~ FRANCES RIDLEY HAVERGAL ~

A prisoner's dying thoughts

Alexander Maclaren (1826-1910) was known in his lifetime as 'the prince of expository preachers'. He was pastor of the Union Chapel, Manchester from 1858 to 1903 and his best known work was Expositions of Holy Scripture.

The following extracts are from a sermon on 2 Timothy 4:6-8:

> For I am already being poured out like a drink offering, and the time has come for my departure. I have fought the good fight, I have finished the race, I have kept the faith. Now there is in store for me the crown of righteousness, which the Lord, the righteous Judge, will award to me on that day — and not only to me, but also to all who have longed for his appearing.

AND NOW the end is near. A prison and the headsman's sword are the world's wages to its best teacher. When Nero is on the throne, the only possible place for Paul is the dungeon opening on to the scaffold. Better to be the martyr than the Caesar!

There is great beauty and force in the expressions which he uses for death here. He... calls it an offering and a departure.

We have first, the metaphor of an *offering*, or more particularly of a *drink offering*, or *libation*, 'I am already being poured out.' No doubt the special reason for the selection of this figure here is Paul's anticipation of a violent death. The shedding of his blood was to be an offering poured out like some costly wine upon the altar, but the power of the figure reaches far beyond that special application of it. We may all make our deaths a sacrifice, an offering to God, for we may yield up our will to God's will, and so turn that last struggle into an act of worship and self surrender. When we recognize his hand, when we submit our wills to his purposes, when 'we live unto the Lord' – if we live – and 'die unto the Lord' (ROMANS 14:8) – if we die – then death will lose all its terror and most of its pain and will become for us what it was to Paul, a true offering up of self in thankful worship. No, we may even say, that so we shall in a certain subordinate sense be 'made conformable unto his death' (PHILIPPIANS 3:10) who committed his spirit into his Father's hands and laid down his life, of his own will. The essential character and far-reaching effects of this sacrifice we cannot imitate, but we can so yield up our wills to God and leave life so willingly and trustfully as that death shall make our sacrifice complete.

Another more familiar and equally striking figure is next used when Paul speaks of the time of his 'departure'… To those who have learned the meaning of Christ's resurrection, and feed their souls on the hopes that it warrants, death is merely a change of place or state, an accident affecting locality, and little more… How strong is the conviction, spoken in that name for death, that the essential life lasts on quite unaltered through it all! How slight the else formidable thing is made! We may change climates, and for the stormy bleakness of life may have the long still days of heaven, but we do not change ourselves…

The one question for us all then will be, 'Have I lived for Christ and by him?' Let it be the one question for us now, and let it be answered, 'Yes.' Then we shall have at the last a calm confidence, equally far removed from presumption and from dread, which will let us look back on life, though it be full of failures and sins, with peace, and forward with humble hope of the reward that we shall receive from his mercy.

If you can humbly say, to me to live is Christ, then is it well. Living by him we may fight and conquer, may win and obtain. Living by him, we may be ready quietly to lie down when the time comes, and may have all the future filled with the blaze of a great hope that glows brighter as the darkness thickens. That peaceful hope will not leave us until consciousness fails. Then, when it has ceased to guide us, Christ himself will lead us, scarcely knowing where we are, through the waters; when we open our half-bewildered eyes in brief wonder, the first thing we see will be his welcoming smile. His voice will say, as a tender surgeon might to a little child waking after an operation, 'It is all over.'

~ ALEXANDER MACLAREN ~

Christ – our hope in death

For twenty-five years, Charlotte Elliott edited an annual Christian devotional. She also compiled a hymnal (including 100 of her own hymns) for the encouragement of seriously ill people. She was able to empathize exactly with how they were feeling, and she exerted a wide and significant ministry in this way. The following verses she entitled, 'For a dying bed':

> CHRIST IS MY HOPE, Christ is my life,
> Christ is my strength, my victory –
>   In this dark hour – this final strife,
>   Through Christ a conqueror I shall be!
> Himself he will beside me stand,
> And save me with his own right hand.
>
> Christ is my treasure, Christ my joy,
> I glory in his name alone,
>   And death each barrier will destroy
>   Which keeps me from that glorious throne,
> Where I shall see him face to face,
> While all his mercies I retrace.

~ CHARLOTTE ELLIOTT ~

'For ever with the Lord!'

James Montgomery (1771-1854) was a writer and newspaper editor who used his position to campaign for a host of good causes, including the abolition of slavery. He was imprisoned for his views at least twice. He wrote more than 400 hymns, several of which are still popular today.

This hymn is based on 1 Thessalonians 4:17:

After that, we who are still alive and are left will be caught up together with them in the clouds to meet the Lord in the air. And so we will be with the Lord for ever.

'FOR EVER with the Lord!'
  Amen, so let it be!
Life from the dead is in that word,
  And immortality.

In longing discontent,
  Absent from him I roam,
Yet nightly pitch my moving tent
  A day's march nearer home.

My Father's house on high,
  Home of my soul, how near
At times to faith's foreseeing eye
  Those golden gates appear!

O how my spirit faints
  To reach the land I love,
The bright inheritance of saints,
  Jerusalem above.

All that I am, have been,
    All that I yet may be,
He sees at once, as he has seen,
    And shall for ever see.

How can I meet his eyes?
    Mine on the cross I cast
And count my life the Saviour's prize;
    Mercy from first to last.

'For ever with the Lord!'
    Father, this is your will:
The promise of that faithful word
    On earth to me fulfil.

Be now at my right hand,
    Then can I never fail;
Uphold me, and I firm shall stand
    Fight, and I must prevail.

So when my final breath
    Shall set me free from pain,
By death I shall escape from death,
    And life eternal gain.

That resurrection word,
    That shout of victory,
Once more: 'For ever with the Lord!'
    Amen, so let it be!

~ JAMES MONTGOMERY ~

A Passion hymn

Paul Gerhardt (1607-1676), a Lutheran pastor, lived during the religious wars in Germany, and he suffered much as a result of the great controversies of the day. He also endured personal hardship: five of his six children died in infancy, and his wife also died prematurely. However, Paul Gerhardt found refuge in writing hymns, despite circumstances 'which would have made most men cry, rather than sing'. His hymns include: 'Commit thou all thy griefs', 'Give to the winds thy fears', and 'All my heart this night rejoices'. His last words were a portion from one of his own hymns:

Him no death has power to kill,
But from many a dreaded ill
Bears his spirit safe away.

O SACRED HEAD! now wounded,
  With grief and shame weighed down,
Now scornfully surrounded
  With thorns, thine only crown;
O sacred head! what glory,
  What bliss till now was thine!
Yet though despised and gory,
  I joy to call thee mine.

O noblest brow, and dearest!
  In other days the world
All feared, when thou appearedst.
  What shame on thee is hurled!

How art thou pale with anguish,
  With sore abuse and scorn;
How does that visage languish,
  Which once was bright as morn.

What thou, my Lord, hast suffered
  Was all for sinners' gain.
Mine, mine was the transgression,
  But thine the deadly pain.
Lo! here I fall, my Saviour,
  'Tis I deserve thy place.
Look on me with thy favour,
  Vouchsafe me to thy grace.

Receive me, my Redeemer,
  My Shepherd, make me thine.
Of every good the fountain,
  Thou art the spring of mine.
Beside thee, Lord, I've taken
  My place – forbid me not!
Hence will I ne'er be shaken,
  Though thou to death be brought.

The joy can ne'er be spoken
  Above all joys beside,
When in thy body broken
  I thus with safety hide.
My Lord of life, desiring
  Thy glory now to see,
Beside the cross expiring,
  I'd breathe my soul to thee.

What language shall I borrow
  To thank thee, dearest Friend,
For this thy dying sorrow,
  Thy pity without end?
Oh! make me thine forever,
  And should I fainting be,
Lord, let me never, never
  Outlive my love to thee.

And when I am departing,
  Oh! part not thou from me.
When mortal pangs are darting,
  Come, Lord, and set me free.
And when my heart must languish
  Amidst the final throe,
Release me from mine anguish
  By thine own pain and woe.

Be near me when I'm dying,
  Oh! show thy cross to me,
And for my succour flying,
  Come, Lord, and set me free.
These eyes, new faith receiving,
  From Jesus shall not move,
For he who dies believing
  Dies safely through thy love.

~ PAUL GERHARDT ~
TRANSLATED BY JAMES W. ALEXANDER
(1804-1859)

AND THEN...
eternity

Following the return of Christ, this earth will be renewed and restored. The bodies of God's people from all ages who have already died will be raised, renewed, and 'reunited' with their spirits which have been in heaven with him. Those who have not died will also be 'changed', and given new bodies. Following the judgement, God's people will live and reign in the new heavens and the new earth for ever.

All of God's wonderful purposes for creation, which were so sadly spoiled by the Fall, will then be fulfilled. At the cross of Christ, every effect of the curse was reversed. During this present age, although Satan is defeated in principle, we still see the evil effects of his activity everywhere in the world. But the new heavens and new earth will be perfect in every way: unspoiled by sin; untouched by Satan.

The coming of the Lord

BROTHERS, we do not want you to be ignorant about those who fall asleep, or to grieve like the rest of men, who have no hope. We believe that Jesus died and rose again and so we believe that God will bring with Jesus those who have fallen asleep in him. According to the Lord's own word, we tell you that we who are still alive, who are left till the coming of the Lord, will certainly not precede those who have fallen asleep. For the Lord himself will come down from heaven, with a loud command, with the voice of the archangel and with the trumpet call of God, and the dead in Christ will rise first. After that, we who are still alive and are left will be caught up together with them in the clouds to meet the Lord in the air. And so we will be with the Lord for ever. Therefore encourage each other with these words.

~ 1 THESSALONIANS 4:13-18 ~

The coming of the King

'BEHOLD, I am coming soon! Blessed is he who keeps the words of the prophecy in this book.'

~ REVELATION 22:7 ~

'BEHOLD, I am coming soon! My reward is with me, and I will give to everyone according to what he has done.'

~ REVELATION 22:12 ~

HE WHO TESTIFIES to these things says, 'Yes, I am coming soon.'
    Amen. Come, Lord Jesus.'

~ REVELATION 22:20 ~

This hymn by Frances Ridley Havergal expresses the longing of God's people for the return of Christ:

THOU ART COMING, O my Saviour!
    Thou art coming, O my King!
In thy beauty all-resplendent,
In thy glory all-transcendent;
    Well may we rejoice and sing!
Coming! in the opening east,
    Herald brightness slowly swells;

Coming! O my glorious Priest,
  Hear we not thy golden bells?

Thou art coming, thou art coming!
  We shall meet thee on thy way;
We shall see thee, we shall know thee,
We shall bless thee, we shall show thee
  All our hearts could never say!
What an anthem that will be,
Ringing out our love to thee,
Pouring out our rapture sweet
At thine own all-glorious feet!

Thou art coming! Rays of glory,
  Through the veil thy death has rent,
Touch the mountain and the river
With a golden glowing quiver,
  Thrill of light and music blent.
Earth is brightened when this gleam
Falls on flower and rock and stream;
Life is brightened when this ray
Falls upon its darkest day.

Not a cloud and not a shadow,
  Not a mist and not a tear,
Not a sin and not a sorrow,
Not a dim and veiled to-morrow,
  For that sunrise grand and clear!
Jesus, Saviour, once with thee,
  Nothing else seems worth a thought!
O how marvellous will be
  All the bliss thy pain hath bought!

Thou art coming! At thy table
  We are witnesses for this,
While remembering hearts thou meetest,
In communion clearest, sweetest,
  Earnest of our coming bliss;
Showing not thy death alone,
  And thy love, exceeding great,
But thy coming and thy throne,
  All for which we long and wait.

Thou art coming! We are waiting
  With a hope that cannot fail;
Asking not the day or hour,
Resting on thy word of power
  Anchored safe within the veil.
Time appointed may be long,
  But the vision must be sure:
Certainty shall make us strong;
  Joyful patience can endure!

Oh, the joy to see thee reigning,
  Thee, my own belovèd Lord!
Every tongue thy name confessing,
Worship, honour, glory, blessing,
  Brought to thee with glad accord!
Thee, my Master and my Friend,
  Vindicated and enthroned!
Unto earth's remotest end
Glorified, adored, and owned!

~ FRANCES RIDLEY HAVERGAL ~

God will be with them

THEN I SAW a new heaven and a new earth, for the first heaven and the first earth had passed away, and there was no longer any sea. I saw the Holy City, the new Jerusalem, coming down out of heaven from God, prepared as a bride beautifully dressed for her husband. And I heard a loud voice from the throne saying, 'Now the dwelling of God is with men, and he will live with them. They will be his people, and God himself will be with them and be their God. He will wipe every tear from their eyes. There will be no more death or mourning or crying or pain, for the old order of things has passed away.'

~ REVELATION 21:1-4 ~

THEN THE ANGEL showed me the river of the water of life, as clear as crystal, flowing from the throne of God and of the Lamb down the middle of the great street of the city. On each side of the river stood the tree of life, bearing twelve crops of fruit, yielding its fruit every month. And the leaves of the tree are for the healing of the nations. No longer will there be any curse. The throne of God and of the Lamb will be in the city, and his servants will serve him. They will see his face, and his name will be on their foreheads. There will be no more night. They will not need the light of a lamp or the light of the sun, for the Lord God will give them light. And they will reign for ever and ever.

~ REVELATION 22:1-5 ~

Judgement: the putting right of all wrongs

The second coming in glory of the Lord Jesus is the great event for which we long. He will come to judge the earth, which, as author Bruce Milne explains, is the ultimate vindication of all God's purposes:

THE LAST JUDGEMENT is a solemn prospect, but we dare not forget that the judgement day is very much more than the banishment of the impenitent. God's judgement means nothing less than the establishing of his just and joyous reign, the putting right of all that has gone wrong, and the liberation of all things from the usurping shadow of evil. It is this perspective that enables the psalmist to *celebrate* God's judgements. 'Let the heavens rejoice, let the earth be glad... let the fields be jubilant... the trees... will sing for joy... before the LORD, for he comes... to judge the earth... and the peoples in his truth' (PSALM 96:11-13). Our hearts have cried with the people of God throughout the ages!

O that you would rend the heavens and come down! Let God be God! Vindicate your name... overthrow the forces of darkness... vanquish the devil and remove him... bring an end to the long night of wrong and evil; an end to exploitation and sin, and wickedness in all its forms... Come Lord Jesus, take your rightful place upon the throne and reign in your glory... Father, hallowed be your name, your kingdom come, your will be done on earth as it is in heaven... Let there be glory to the Father, and the Son and the Holy Spirit, one God for ever!

The coming of the judgement day is the answer to these prayers, and the means of their being answered. It is also therefore a day for rejoicing. This is the way it is consistently viewed in the book of Revelation, where the redeemed are regularly exhibited celebrating the just judgements of God.

We give thanks to you, Lord God Almighty, the One who is and who was, because you have taken your great power and have begun to reign. The nations were angry; and your wrath has come. The time has come for judging the dead, and for rewarding your servants the prophets and your saints and those who reverence your name, both small and great – and for destroying those who destroy the earth [REVELATION 11:17-18].

All history is moving to a climax. At the centre of it will be the last judgement. It will occur 'before the throne of God'. It will be universal: every human person from all the ages of history will be there. It will call in evidence all human deeds. The only hope of acquittal will lie in our names being entered in 'the Lamb's book of life'. The alternative, for those not acquitted, is overwhelmingly solemn – being consigned to hell. The last judgement is God's final triumph over all his foes, and therefore a major ground for his praise.

~ BRUCE MILNE ~

God's gracious purpose for the whole cosmos

'REPENT, THEN, and turn to God, so that your sins may be wiped out, that times of refreshing may come from the Lord, and that he may send the Christ, who has been appointed for you – even Jesus. He must remain in heaven until the time comes for God to restore everything, as he promised long ago through his holy prophets.'

~ ACTS 3:19-21 ~

THAT DAY will bring about the destruction of the heavens by fire, and the elements will melt in the heat. But in keeping with his promise we are looking forward to a new heaven and a new earth, the home of righteousness.

~ 2 PETER 3:12-13 ~

AND HE made known to us the mystery of his will according to his good pleasure, which he purposed in Christ, to be put into effect when the times will have reached their fulfilment – to bring all things in heaven and on earth together under one head, even Christ.

~ EPHESIANS 1:9-10 ~

FOR GOD was pleased to have all his fulness dwell in him, and through him to reconcile to himself all things, whether things on earth or things in heaven, by making peace through his blood, shed on the cross.

~ COLOSSIANS 1:19-20 ~

THE GOAL OF REDEMPTION is nothing less than the renewal of the cosmos... Since man's fall into sin affected not only himself but the rest of creation, redemption from sin must also involve the totality of creation... The work of Christ, therefore, is not just to save certain individuals, not even to save an innumerable throng of blood-bought people. The total work of Christ is nothing less than to redeem this entire creation from the effects of sin. That purpose will not be accomplished until God has ushered in the new earth, until *Paradise Lost* has become *Paradise Regained*...

~ ANTHONY A. HOEKEMA ~

The biblical hope
of bodily resurrection

Geerhardus Vos comments that the word 'spiritual' ought to be capitalized in the following text. 'Spiritual' here does not mean 'non-material'. It means Holy Spirit controlled. We leave behind our frail, sinful bodies, and have glorious new sinless bodies, totally directed by the Spirit.

So WILL IT BE with the resurrection of the dead. The body that is sown is perishable, it is raised imperishable; it is sown in dishonour, it is raised in glory; it is sown in weakness, it is raised in power; it is sown a natural body, it is raised a spiritual body. If there is a natural body, there is also a spiritual body.

~ I CORINTHIANS 15:42-44 ~

LISTEN, I tell you a mystery: We will not all sleep, but we will all be changed — in a flash, in the twinkling of an eye, at the last trumpet. For the trumpet will sound, the dead will be raised imperishable, and we will be changed. For the perishable must clothe itself with the imperishable, and the mortal with immortality.

~ I CORINTHIANS 15:51-53 ~

AND AFTER my skin has been destroyed, yet in my flesh I will see God.

~ JOB 19:26 ~

MULTITUDES WHO SLEEP in the dust of the earth will awake: some to everlasting life, others to shame and everlasting contempt. Those who are wise will shine like the brightness of the heavens, and those who lead many to righteousness, like the stars for ever and ever.

~ DANIEL 12:2-3 ~

FOR THE LORD himself will come down from heaven, with a loud command, with the voice of the archangel and with the trumpet call of God, and the dead in Christ will rise first.

~ I THESSALONIANS 4:16 ~

BUT OUR CITIZENSHIP is in heaven. And we eagerly await a Saviour from there, the Lord Jesus Christ, who, by the power that enables him to bring everything under his control, will transform our lowly bodies so that they will be like his glorious body.

~ PHILIPPIANS 3:20-21 ~

IF THE RESURRECTION BODY were nonmaterial or non-physical, the devil would have won a great victory, since God would then have been compelled to change human beings with physical bodies such as he had created into creatures of a different sort, without physical bodies (like the angels). Then it would indeed seem that matter had become intrinsically evil so that it had to be banished... But matter is not evil; it is part of God's good creation. Therefore the goal of God's redemption is the resurrection of the physical body, and the creation of a new earth on which his redeemed people can live and serve God forever with glorified bodies. Thus the universe will not be destroyed but renewed, and God will win the victory.

~ ANTHONY A. HOEKEMA ~

Old Testament prophecies about the new heavens and earth

The prophetic perspective of the Old Testament has often been compared to looking at a massive mountain range. Peak after peak may initially appear to be quite close together. In fact, they may be hundreds of miles apart. From the Old Testament perspective, the future often blended into one great 'mountain range': the restoration of the Jews from the Babylonian captivity, the first coming of the Messiah, the pouring out of the Spirit at Pentecost and the second coming of the Messiah. Many of the prophecies have 'layers' of meaning, and can apply to one, more, or all of those events in salvation history. The prophecies below reach their 'fullest and final' fulfilment in the establishment of the new heavens and the new earth after the second coming of Christ. But they also point to the blessings of the present gospel age.

THE LORD SAYS to my Lord:
  'Sit at my right hand
until I make your enemies
  a footstool for your feet.'

The LORD will extend your mighty
  sceptre from Zion;
  you will rule in the midst of your enemies.

~ PSALM 110:1-2 ~

ASK OF ME,
    and I will make the nations your inheritance,
    the ends of the earth your possession.

~ PSALM 2:8 ~

IN THE LAST DAYS

the mountain of the LORD's temple
        will be established
    as chief among the mountains;
it will be raised above the hills,
and all nations will stream to it.

Many peoples will come and say,

'Come, let us go up to the mountain of the LORD,
    to the house of the God of Jacob.
He will teach us his ways,
    so that we may walk in his paths.'
The law will go out from Zion,
    the word of the LORD from Jerusalem.
He will judge between the nations
    and will settle disputes for many peoples.
They will beat their swords into ploughshares
    and their spears into pruning hooks.
Nation will not take up sword against nation,
    nor will they train for war any more.

~ ISAIAH 2:2-4 ~

THE WOLF will live with the lamb,
  the leopard will lie down with the goat,
the calf and the lion and the yearling together;
  and a little child will lead them.
The cow will feed with the bear,
  their young will lie down together,
  and the lion will eat straw like the ox.
The infant will play near the hole of the cobra,
  and the young child put his hand into the
    viper's nest.
They will neither harm nor destroy
  on all my holy mountain,
for the earth will be full of the
    knowledge of the LORD
  as the waters cover the sea.

~ ISAIAH 11:6-9 ~

ON THIS MOUNTAIN the LORD Almighty will prepare
  a feast of rich food for all peoples,
a banquet of aged wine –
  the best of meats and the finest of wines.
On this mountain he will destroy
  the shroud that enfolds all peoples,
the sheet that covers all nations;
  he will swallow up death for ever.
The Sovereign LORD will wipe away the tears
  from all faces;
he will remove the disgrace of his people
  from all the earth. The LORD has spoken.

~ ISAIAH 25:6-8 ~

'Behold, I will create
    new heavens and a new earth.
The former things will not be remembered,
    nor will they come to mind.
But be glad and rejoice for ever
    in what I will create,
for I will create Jerusalem to be a delight
    and its people a joy.
I will rejoice over Jerusalem
    and take delight in my people;
the sound of weeping and of crying
    will be heard in it no more.

Never again will there be in it
    an infant who lives but a few days,
    or an old man who does not live out his years;
he who dies at a hundred
    will be thought a mere youth;
he who fails to reach a hundred
    will be considered accursed.
They will build houses and dwell in them;
    they will plant vineyards and eat their fruit.
No longer will they build houses and others
        live in them,
    or plant and others eat.
For as the days of a tree,
    so will be the days of my people;
my chosen ones will long enjoy
    the works of their hands.
They will not toil in vain
    or bear children doomed to misfortune;
for they will be a people blessed by the Lord,

they and their descendants with them.
Before they call I will answer;
    while they are still speaking I will hear.
The wolf and the lamb will feed together,
    and the lion will eat straw like the ox,
    but dust will be the serpent's food.
They will neither harm nor destroy
    on all my holy mountain,' says the LORD.

~ ISAIAH 65:17-25 ~

'AS THE NEW HEAVENS and the new earth that I make will endure before me', declares the Lord, 'so will your name and descendants endure. From one New Moon to another and from one Sabbath to another, all mankind will come and bow down before me', says the Lord.

~ ISAIAH 66:22-23 ~

The glories of the
renewed universe

'The nations will walk by its light, and the kings of the earth will bring their splendour into it. On no day will its gates ever be shut, for there will be no night there. The glory and honour of the nations will be brought into it' (Revelation 21:24-26).

ONE COULD SAY that, according to these words, the inhabitants of the new earth will include people who attained great prominence and exercised great power on the present earth... One could also say that whatever people have done on this earth which glorified God will be remembered in the life to come (see REVELATION 14:13). But more must be said. Is it too much to say that, according to these verses, the unique contributions of each nation to the life of the present earth will enrich the life of the new earth? Shall we then perhaps inherit the best products of culture and art which this earth has produced? Hendrikus Berkhof suggests that whatever has been of value in this present life, whatever has contributed to 'the liberation of human existence', will be retained and added to on the new earth. In support of this thought he quotes the following sentence from Abraham Kuyper: 'If an endless field of human knowledge and of human ability is now being formed by all that takes place in order to make the visible world and material nature subject to us, and if we know that this dominion of ours over nature will be complete in eternity, we may conclude that the knowledge and dominion we have gained over nature here can and will be of continual significance, even in the kingdom of glory.'

The doctrine of the new earth should give us hope, courage, and optimism in a day of widespread despair. Though evil is rampant in this world, it is comforting to know that Christ has won the final victory... As citizens of God's kingdom, we may not just write off the present earth as a total loss, or rejoice in its deterioration. We must indeed be working for a better world now. Our efforts to bring the kingdom of Christ into fuller manifestation are of eternal significance. Our Christian life today, our struggles against sin – both individual and institutional – our mission work, our attempt to develop and promote a distinctively Christian culture, have value not only for this world but even for the world to come.

As we live on this earth, we are preparing for life on God's new earth. Through our kingdom service, the building materials for that new earth are now being gathered. Bibles are being translated, peoples are being evangelized, believers are being renewed, and cultures are being transformed. Only eternity will reveal the full significance of what has been done for Christ here.

At the beginning of history God created the heavens and the earth. At the end of history we see the new heavens and the new earth, which will far surpass in splendour all that we have seen before. At the centre of history is the Lamb that was slain, the first-born from the dead, and the Ruler of the kings of the earth. Some day we shall cast all our crowns before him, 'lost in wonder, love, and praise'.

~ ANTHONY A. HOEKEMA ~

Will we know each other in the new creation?

JESUS SAID: I tell you, use worldly wealth to gain friends for yourselves, so that when it is gone, you will be welcomed into eternal dwellings.

~ LUKE 16:9 ~

ACCORDING to LUKE 16:9 the friends whom we make for ourselves by our material gifts will welcome us into the mansions of heaven. The sick whom we have visited, the bereaved with whom we have sympathized, the heathen for whom we have been instruments unto salvation will as it were be standing in the vestibule of heaven in order to receive their benefactors into their circle, so as together to glorify the One who is the source of every blessing. This surely implies recognition and resumption of fellowship.

~ WILLIAM HENDRIKSEN ~

WHEN I LOOK in the faces of the precious people of God, and think of that day, what a refreshing thought it is! He who commands us so to love them now, will give us leave to love them then, when he has made them much more lovely. I know that Christ is all in all; and that it is the presence of God that makes heaven to be heaven. But yet it much sweetens the thoughts of that place to me that there are there such a multitude of my most dear and precious friends in Christ.

~ RICHARD BAXTER ~

THE HOPE to see one another on the other side of the grave is entirely natural, genuinely human, and also in harmony in Scripture… It is true that the joy of heaven consists primarily in fellowship with Christ, [but] it also consists in fellowship of believers with each other… Jesus himself pictures the joy of heaven under the symbolism of a banquet where all will sit at the table with Abraham, Isaac and Jacob (MATTHEW 8:11; LUKE 13:28).

~HERMAN BAVINCK ~

Continuity in the new creation

Some fear that they will lose personal identity in the new heavens and the new earth. C.S. Lewis comments on Revelation 2:17, ' I will also give him a white stone with a new name written on it, known only to him who receives it.'

WHAT CAN BE more a man's own than this new name which even in eternity remains a secret between God and him? And what shall we take this secrecy to mean? Surely, that each of the redeemed shall for ever know and praise some one aspect of the divine beauty better than any other creature can. Why else were individuals created, but that God, loving all things infinitely should love each differently?

~ C. S. LEWIS ~

Some wonder whether the new heavens and the new earth will have less to offer than the present earth.

IF PLANTS and animals shared in man's Fall, will he [God] not want them to share in man's redemption and glory? If plants and animals were meant to be man's companions and joy in the past, why not in the future? What would planet earth be without them?

~ EDMUND J. FORTMAN ~

It will not, then, be a totally different world, but a renewed one:

THE WORLD into which we shall enter... is therefore not another world; it is this world, this heaven, this earth; both, however, passed away and renewed. It is these forests, these fields, these cities, these streets, these people, that will be the scene of redemption. At present they are battlefields, full of the strife and sorrow of the not yet accomplished consummation; then they will lie fields of victory, fields of harvest, where out of seed that was sown with tears, the everlasting sheaves will be reaped and brought home.

~ EDWARD THURNEYSEN ~

Service in the new creation

BUT WE MUST NOT define worship too narrowly, for our entire existence will be worship. Heaven, as we have seen, will be a physical as well as a spiritual reality, 'a new heaven and a new earth' (REVELATION 21:1). We will be stewards of this new earth, managing it for God's glory. The writer to the Hebrews quotes PSALM 8 in reminding us that God made man ruler of the earth (HEBREWS 2:7-8). This position of authority, diminished by the Fall, has not yet been restored fully, for 'now we do not yet see all things put under him. But we see Jesus... crowned with glory and honour' (HEBREWS 2:8-9). The implication is clear. We do not yet see all things put under man, but we will. Because Jesus has gone before us on our behalf and the day is coming when complete stewardship of creation will be returned to us and we will sing the psalm with new meaning: 'What is man that you are mindful of him... You have made him to have dominion over the works of your hands; you have put all things under his feet... O LORD, our Lord, how excellent is your name in all the earth!' (PSALM 8:4,6,9).

In this new world we will be given remarkable new tasks. Thrilling avenues of service will open before us, calling for the use of all our gifts and talents, many unsuspected or undeveloped in our present existence. 'The reason, the intellectual curiosity, the imagination, the aesthetic instincts, the holy affections, the social affinities, the inexhaustible resources of strength and power native to the human soul, must all find in heaven exercise and satisfaction.'[1] Throughout eternity we will live full, truly human lives, exploring and managing God's creation to his glory. Fascinating vistas will unfold before us as we learn to serve God in a renewed universe. 'Every legitimate activity of (new) creaturely life will be included within the life of worship of God's people.'[2]

It is challenging to reflect that the greater our faithfulness now, the more extensive and fulfilling our heavenly responsibilities will be. 'Well done, good and faithful servant; you have been faithful over a few things, I will make you ruler over many things' (MATTHEW 25:23). Christ rewards us for work well done by entrusting more responsibility to us.

~ EDWARD DONNELLY ~

'Then, Lord, shall I fully know'

The hymn opposite perfectly sums up Robert Murray M'Cheyne's conviction that his salvation was all of grace, and that only in heaven would we fully realize the length and breadth and height of the love of Christ to us.

AND I PRAY that you, being rooted and established in love, may have power, together with all the saints, to grasp how wide and long and high and deep is the love of Christ, and to know this love that surpasses knowledge – that you may be filled to the measure of all the fulness of God.

~ EPHESIANS 3:17-19

FOR I AM convinced that neither death nor life, neither angels nor demons, neither the present nor the future, nor any powers, neither height nor depth, nor anything else in all creation, will be able to separate us from the love of God that is in Christ Jesus our Lord.

~ ROMANS 8:38-39 ~

'WHEN THIS passing world is done,
  When has sunk yon radiant sun,
When I stand with Christ on high,
  Looking o'er life's history,
Then, Lord, shall I fully know,
  Not till then, how much I owe.

When I stand before the throne,
  Dressed in beauty not my own,
When I see thee as thou art,
  Love thee with unsinning heart,
Then, Lord, shall I fully know,
  Not till then, how much I owe.

When the praise of heaven I hear,
  Loud as thunders to the ear,
Loud as many waters' noise,
  Sweet as harp's melodious voice,
Then, Lord, shall I fully know,
  Not till then, how much I owe.

Chosen, not for good in me,
  Wakened up from wrath to flee,
Hidden in the Saviour's side,
  By the Spirit sanctified,
Teach me, Lord, on earth to show
  By my love how much I owe.

~ ROBERT MURRAY MᶜCHEYNE ~

Heaven, a world of love

Jonathan Edwards (1703-1758), an influential American preacher during the Great Awakening, was regarded as the foremost theologian of his time. Among his many writings is a detailed exposition of 1 Corinthians 13, entitled Charity and its Fruits. *In the section on verses 8-10, 'Love never fails...', Edwards launched into one of the most exquisite descriptions of heaven ever penned.*

GOD, considered with respect to his essence, is everywhere. But heaven is his dwelling-place above all other places in the universe. All those places in which he was said to dwell of old, were but types of this. Heaven is a part of creation that God has built to be the place of his glorious presence. It is his abode for ever. Here will he gloriously manifest himself for all eternity.

And this renders heaven a world of love. God is the fountain of love, as the sun is the fountain of light. And therefore the glorious presence of God in heaven, fills heaven with love, as the sun, placed in the midst of the visible heavens in a clear day, fills the world with light. The apostle tells us that 'God is love'; and therefore, seeing he is an infinite being, it follows that he is an infinite fountain of love. Seeing he is an all-sufficient being, it follows that he is a full and overflowing, and inexhaustible fountain of love. And in that he is an unchangeable and eternal being, he is an unchangeable and eternal fountain of love.

Heaven, the dwelling of the triune God

There dwells God the Father, who is the Father of mercies,

and so the Father of love, who so loved the world as to give his only-begotten Son to die for it. There dwells Christ, the Lamb of God, the Prince of peace and of love, who so loved the world that he shed his blood, and poured out his soul unto death for men. He is the great Mediator, through whom all the divine love is expressed toward men, and by whom the fruits of that love have been purchased, and through whom they are communicated, and through whom love is imparted to the hearts of all God's people. Christ is there in both his natures, the human and the divine, sitting on the same throne with the Father. And there dwells the Holy Spirit — the Spirit of divine love — in whom the very essence of God, as it were, flows out, and is breathed forth in love, and by whose immediate influence all holy love is shed abroad in the hearts of all the saints on earth and in heaven.

Love is always mutual in heaven

As the saints will love God with an inconceivable fervour of heart, and to the utmost of their capacity, so they will know that he has loved them from all eternity, and still loves them, and will continue to love them for ever. God will then gloriously manifest himself to them, and they shall know that all that happiness and glory which they are possessed of, are the fruits of his love. And with the same ardour and fervency will the saints love the Lord Jesus Christ and their love will be accepted; and they shall know that he has loved them with a faithful, yea even with a dying love. They shall then appreciate the great love of Christ so much more fully than now. They will understand more of his dying love. Christ will open to their view the great fountain of love in his heart for them, in a way beyond our comprehension now.

Hereby the love of the saints to God and Christ is seen to be reciprocated, and that declaration fulfilled, 'I love them that love me'; and though the love of God to them cannot properly be called the return of love, because he loved them first, yet the sight of his love will, on that very account, the more fill them with joy and admiration, and love to him.

Love between the saints in heaven

There shall be no such thing as flattery or dissimulation in heaven, but there perfect sincerity shall reign through all and in all. Every one will be just what he seems to be, and will really have all the love that he seems to have. It will not be as in this world, where comparatively few things are what they seem to be, and where professions are often made lightly and without meaning; but there, every expression of love shall come from the bottom of the heart, and all that is professed shall be really and truly felt.

The saints shall know that God loves them, and they shall never doubt the greatness of his love and they shall have no doubt of the love of all their fellow-inhabitants in heaven. The saints shall have no fear that the love of God will ever abate towards them, or that Christ will not continue always to love them with unabated tenderness and affection. And they shall have no jealousy one of another, but shall know that by divine grace the mutual love that exists between them shall never decay nor change.

The saints in heaven shall have no difficulty in expressing all their love. Their souls being on fire with holy love, shall not be like a fire pent up but like a flame uncovered and at liberty. Their spirits being winged with love, shall have no weight upon them to hinder their flight. There shall be no want of strength or activity, nor any want of words wherewith to praise the object of their affection. Nothing shall hinder them from communing with God, and praising and serving him just as their love inclines them to do. Love naturally desires to express itself; and in heaven the love of the saints shall be at full liberty to express itself as it desires, whether it be towards God or to created beings.

There shall be none there to tempt any to dislike or hatred; no busybodies or malicious adversaries, to make misrepresentations or create misunderstandings or spread abroad any evil reports, but every being and every thing shall conspire to promote love, and the full enjoyment of love. Heaven itself, the place of habitation, is a garden of pleasures, a heavenly paradise fitted in all respects for an abode of heavenly love; a place where they may have sweet society and perfect enjoyment of each other's love. None are unsociable, or distant from each other. The petty distinctions of this world do not draw lines in the society of heaven, but all meet in the equality of holiness and of holy love.

All things in heaven do also remarkably shew forth the beauty and loveliness of God and Christ, and have the brightness and sweetness of divine love upon them. The very light that shines in and fills that world is the light of love, for it is the shining of the glory of the Lamb of God, that most wonderful influence of lamb-like meekness and love that fills the heavenly Jerusalem with light. 'The city had no need of the sun, neither of the moon, to shine in it; for the glory of God did lighten it, and the Lamb is the light thereof' (REVELATION 21:23). The glory that is about him that reigns in heaven is so radiant and sweet that it is compared (REVELATION 4:3) to 'a rainbow round about the throne, in sight like unto an emerald'; and it is the rainbow that is so often used in the Old Testament as the fit token of God's love and grace manifested in his covenant. The light of the new Jerusalem, which is the light of God's glory, is said to be like a jasper stone, clear as crystal (REVELATION 21:11), thus signifying the greatest preciousness and beauty; and as to its continuance, it is said there is no night there but only an endless and glorious day.

Living in the light of heaven

Let what we have heard of the land of love stir us all up to turn our faces toward it. As we anticipate heaven, should we not long to be there? Should we not press towards it with resolution? How wonderful to hear of such a world of perfect peace and holy love, and to know that it is we who have the opportunity to come to it, and spend an eternity in its joys!

Set your heart on heaven that world of love! Press toward that better country where all is kindness and holy affection.

How to seek heaven

First   Don't set your heart on the things of this world as your chief good.

Second Turn your thoughts and affections towards that world of love, and towards the God of love that dwells there, and towards the saints and angels that are at Christ's right hand. Commune much with God and Christ in prayer, and think often of all that is in heaven.

Third   Be content to pass through all difficulties in the way to heaven. What is it all in comparison with the sweet rest that is at your journey's end?

Fourth In all your way let your eye be fixed on Jesus, who has gone to heaven as your forerunner.

Fifth   Live a life of love – of love to God, and love to men.

Then the windows of heaven shall be opened, so that its glorious light shall shine in upon your soul. And this will be assurance that you are on the way there! Being prepared, by grace, for the inheritance of the saints in light, after a short time, you shall be with them in their blessedness for ever. Happy, thrice happy those who shall thus be found faithful to the end, and then shall be welcomed to the joy of their Lord! There 'they shall hunger no more, neither thirst any more; neither shall the sun light on them, nor any heat. For the Lamb which is in the midst of the throne shall feed them, and lead them to living fountains of waters, and God shall wipe away all tears from their eyes.'

~ JONATHAN EDWARDS ~

'The dawn of heaven breaks'

The life of Samuel Rutherford

'The sands of time are sinking, the dawn of heaven breaks' is one of the best-loved hymns about heaven in the English language. The six verses found in hymn-books are taken from a nineteen-verse poem, 'In Immanuel's Land'. The author was Anne Ross Cousin (1824-1906), a hymn-writer and minister's wife. The poem was closely based on the writings of Samuel Rutherford (c. 1600-1661), a Scottish Presbyterian minister, best known for his book Lex Rex, an attack on absolute monarchy. The phrases in virtually every line can be found in his letters and other writings.

From 1627 to 1636 Rutherford ministered at Anwoth, a tiny hamlet overlooking the Solway Firth. Early in his ministry his two infant children died, and then his wife died in 1630 after a long and agonizing illness.

These were difficult and dangerous times for any ministers who were not willing to submit to State control of the Church. Because of his Calvinist convictions, Rutherford was banned from preaching and exiled to Aberdeen from 1636 to 1638. These were hard years: having lost his family, he had regarded preaching to be his 'poor man's one eye', and now that too was taken from him. When freed, he became professor at St Mary's College, St Andrews. He remarried in 1640. During the Commonwealth period he took part in the famous Westminster Assembly in London. While in London, he and his second wife, Jean, suffered the loss of both their children. Heartbroken, he commented that the Husbandman has a right to pick his roses and lilies in the early summer months. (Of the seven children

Jean bore to Samuel, only one daughter survived). Such bereavements forced an eternal perspective: 'Build your nest on no tree here' he advised a friend, Lady Kenmure, when her first child died (see verse 2).

The poem appears here in its entirety. Every verse is pervaded with a passionate love for Christ and longing for 'love's own country' (verse 7). Rutherford's preaching was always characterized by an extraordinary devotion to the person of Christ. One hearer confessed he thought the minister 'would have flown out of the pulpit when he came to speak of Christ, 'the Rose of Sharon' (see verse 3). His letters, too, breathe out a constant longing and love for the Lord. 'I find Christ's absence to be love's sickness and love's death. The wind that bloweth from the heavens where my Lord Jesus reigneth is sweet-smelled, soft, joyful, as heartsome to a soul burnt with absence' (verses 3 and 8).

Rutherford experienced intense suffering, but the presence of Christ and the prospect of heaven shone light into his dark times (verse 6). The 'sea-beat prison' is Aberdeen, where Rutherford's movements were restricted and, worst of all, he was prohibited from preaching. During his exile he wrote to a friend of his longing to preach again, asking if representation could not be made for his return to his parish. 'But if that never be, thank God, Anwoth is not heaven, preaching is not Christ, I hope to wait on!' (verse 6).

Anwoth, the country parish where Rutherford spent his happiest years, is mentioned in verses 6, 9 and 10. While in exile he wrote: 'I often think the sparrows are blessed who may resort to the house at Anwoth from which I am banished' (see verse 9). He had an absolute passion to see people come to know Christ. 'Take as many to heaven with you as you are able to draw!' he wrote to one friend (see verse 10).

Verses 14 and 18 allude to the bitter persecution he endured.

His preaching and writing were banned, but he looked forward to Christ's vindication, when 'judgement shines like noonday in Immanuel's land'.

From the moment Charles II was restored in 1660, Rutherford was a marked man. All copies of Lex Rex *were gathered together for public burnings in London and Edinburgh. After all, it taught that unlimited sovereignty belongs to God alone — a treasonable teaching! Its author was dismissed from his posts in both Church and University. In the spring of 1661 messengers were sent to call Rutherford before Parliament on a charge of treason. By now he was dying, and absorbed with his Saviour. He was often heard to exclaim 'My blessed Master! My kingly King!' When the messengers arrived he replied simply: 'Tell them that I have a summons already from a superior Judge and judiciary.' It had come from his 'kingly King':*

> *They've summoned me before them,*
> *   But there I cannot come, —*
> *My Lord says 'Come up hither,'*
> *   My Lord says 'Welcome Home!'*
> *My kingly King, at his white throne,*
> *   My presence doth command,*
> *Where glory – glory dwelleth*
> *   In Immanuel's land.*

As he grew weaker, he lay, simply looking forward to being with Christ. 'I shall shine', he was heard to say. 'I shall see him as he is; I shall see him reign, and all the fair company with him... Mine eyes shall see my Redeemer... Let my Lord's name be exalted; and if he will, let my name be ground to pieces that he may be all in all. If he should slay me ten thousand times ten thousand times, I'll trust!' Once or twice he cried out for 'a well

tuned harp', as if already longing to join the praise of heaven
(see verse 12). And, as he finally sank into unconsciousness he
whispered over and over again: 'glory to him in Immanuel's land!'

In Immanuel's Land

1 The sands of time are sinking,
   The dawn of heaven breaks,
The summer morn I've sighed for,
   The fair sweet morn awakes:
Dark, dark hath been the midnight,
   But dayspring is at hand,
And glory – glory dwelleth
   In Immanuel's land.

2 Oh! well it is for ever,
   Oh! well for evermore,
My nest hung in no forest
   Of all this death-doom'd shore:
Yea, let the vain world vanish,
   As from the ship the strand,
And glory – glory dwelleth
   In Immanuel's land.

3 There the Red Rose of Sharon
   Unfolds its heartsome bloom,
And fills the air of heaven
   With ravishing perfume: –
Oh! to behold it blossom,
   While by its fragrance fann'd
Where glory – glory dwelleth
   In Immanuel's land.

4 The King there in his beauty,
   Without a veil, is seen:
It were a well spent journey,
   Though seven deaths lay between.
The Lamb, with his fair army,
   Doth on Mount Zion stand,
And glory – glory dwelleth
   In Immanuel's land.

5 Oh! Christ he is the Fountain,
   The deep sweet well of love!
The streams on earth I've tasted,
   More deep I'll drink above:
There, to an ocean fulness,
   His mercy doth expand,
And glory – glory dwelleth
   In Immanuel's land.

6 E'en Anwoth was not heaven –
   E'en preaching was not Christ;
And in my sea-beat prison
   My Lord and I held tryst:
And aye my murkiest storm cloud
   Was by a rainbow spann'd
Caught from the glory dwelling
   In Immanuel's land.

7 But that he built a heaven
   Of his surpassing love,
A little new Jerusalem,
   Like to the one above, –

'Lord, take me o'er the water',
   Had been my loud demand,
'Take me to love's own country,
   Unto Immanuel's land.'

8 But flowers need night's cool darkness
   The moonlight and the dew;
So Christ, from one who loved it,
   His shining oft withdrew;
And then for cause of absence,
   My troubled soul I scann'd –
But glory, shadeless, shineth
   In Immanuel's land.

9 The little birds of Anwoth
   I used to count them blest, –
Now, beside happier altars
   I go to build my nest:
O'er these there broods no silence,
   No graves around them stand,
For glory, deathless, dwelleth
   In Immanuel's land.

10 Fair Anwoth by the Solway,
   To me thou still art dear!
E'en from the verge of heaven
   I drop for thee a tear.
Oh! if one soul from Anwoth
   Meet me at God's right hand,
My heaven will be two heavens,
   In Immanuel's land.

11   I have wrestled on toward heaven,
   'Gainst storm, and wind, and tide: —
Now, like a weary traveller,
   That leaneth on his guide,
Amid the shades of evening,
   While sinks life's ling'ring sand,
I hail the glory dawning
   From Immanuel's land.

12   Deep water cross'd life's pathway,
   The hedge of thorns was sharp;
Now these lie all behind me —
   Oh! for a well tuned harp!
Oh! to join 'Hallelujah'
   With yon triumphant band,
Who sing, where glory dwelleth,
   In Immanuel's land.

13   With mercy and with judgement
   My web of time he wove,
And aye the dews of sorrow
   Were lustered with his love.
I'll bless the hand that guided,
   I'll bless the heart that plann'd,
When throned where glory dwelleth
   In Immanuel's land.

14   Soon shall the cup of glory
   Wash down earth's bitterest woes,
Soon shall the desert briar
   Break into Eden's rose:

The curse shall change to blessing –
  The name on earth that's bann'd,
Be graven on the white stone
  In Immanuel's land.

15 Oh! I am my Beloved's,
  And my Beloved is mine!
He brings a poor vile sinner
  Into his 'house of wine'.
I stand upon his merit,
  I know no other stand,
Not e'en where glory dwelleth
  In Immanuel's land.

16 I shall sleep sound in Jesus
  Fill'd with his likeness rise,
To live and to adore him,
  To see him with these eyes
'Tween me and resurrection
  But paradise doth stand;
Then – then for glory dwelling
  In Immanuel's land!

17 The bride eyes not her garment
  But her dear Bridegroom's face;
I will not gaze at glory,
  But on my King of grace –
Not at the crown he giveth,
  But on his piercèd hand:
The Lamb is all the glory
  Of Immanuel's land.

18 I have borne scorn and hatred,
    I have borne wrong and shame,
Earth's proud ones have reproach'd me,
    For Christ's thrice blessed name: –
Where God is seal set fairest
    They've stamp'd their foulest brand;
But judgement shines like noonday
    In Immanuel's land.

19 They've summoned me before them,
    But there I may not come, –
My Lord says, 'Come up hither',
    My Lord says, 'Welcome home!'
My kingly King, at his white throne,
    My presence doth command,
Where glory – glory dwelleth
    In Immanuel's land.

~ ANNE ROSS COUSIN ~
BASED ON THE LIFE AND WRITINGS
OF SAMUEL RUTHERFORD

Notes

Many of the older quotes have been slightly abridged and modernized. References are only given where necessary for recent works. The older works are available in many different editions.

Anticipating heaven

Physical healing is not always the will of God (pages 16-17). Taken from *Grace grows best in winter* by Margaret Clarkson (Grand Rapids: Eerdmans Publishing Co., 1984), 33-35. Copyright © 1984 by Margaret Clarkson. Used by permission of Eerdmans Publishing Company, www.eerdmans.com.

Sleeplessness (pages 24-25). Taken from *Grace grows best in winter* by Margaret Clarkson (Grand Rapids: Eerdmans Publishing Co., 1984), 117-121. Copyright © 1984 by Margaret Clarkson. Used by permission of Eerdmans Publishing Company, www.eerdmans.com.

Illness and our spiritual life (pages 28-29). Taken from 'In the Arena' by Isobel Kuhn, included in *The Isobel Kuhn Omnibus* (Carlisle: OM Publishing, 2000), 228-229.

My journey into Alzheimer's disease (pages 50-53). Taken from *My Journey in Alzheimer's Disease* by Robert Davis (Carol Stream: Tyndale House Publishers, 1989), 21, 46, 90-91, 107-111, 120. Copyright © 1989 by Robert Davis. Used by permission of Tyndale House Publishers, Inc., www.tyndale.com.

And then... eternity

Judgement: the putting right of all wrongs (pages 102-103). Taken from *The Message of Heaven and Hell* by Bruce Milne (Nottingham: Inter-Varsity Press, 2002), 306-308.

God's gracious purpose for the whole cosmos (page 105). Taken from *The Bible and the Future* by Anthony A. Hoekema (Grand Rapids: Eerdmans Publishing Co., 1994), 32, 275.

The biblical hope of bodily resurrection (pages 106-108). Geerhardus Vos quoted in *The Bible and the Future* by Anthony A. Hoekema (Grand Rapids: Eerdmans Publishing Co., 1994), 66. Page 108, by Anthony Hoekema, *op. cit*, 250.

The glories of the renewed universe (pages 114-115). Anthony Hoekema, *op. cit.*, 285-287. Reference to Hendrikus Berkhof from *Christ the Meaning of History* (Grand Rapids: Baker Book House, 1979), 191-192; see also 188-191. Abraham Kuyper is quoted in Berkhof, *op. cit*, 191.

Will we know each other in the new creation? (page 116). Taken from *The Bible and the Life Hereafter* by William Hendrikson (Grand Rapids: Baker Book House, 1959), 66-67.

Continuity in the new creation (pages 118-119). C. S. Lewis, *The Problem of Pain* (New York: Macmillan, 1962), 149-150. Edmund J. Fortman, *Everlasting Life*, 311; quoted in John Gilmore, *Probing Heaven: Key Questions on the*

Hereafter (Grand Rapids: Baker Book House, 1989), 123. Edward Thurneysen, quoted in Anthony A. Hoekema, *The Bible and the Future* (Grand Rapids: Eerdmans Publishing Co., 1994), 281.

Service in the new creation (pages 120-121). Taken from *Biblical Teachings on the Doctrines of Heaven and Hell* by Edward Donnelly (Edinburgh: The Banner of Truth Trust, 2002), 123-124. Used by permission of The Banner of Trust Trust, www.banneroftruth.co.uk. Footnote 1: A. A. Hodge, *Evangelical Theology* (Edinburgh: The Banner of Truth Trust, 1977), 400. Footnote 2: Cornelis P. Venema, *The Promise of the Future* (Edinburgh: The Banner of Truth Trust, 2000), 478.

Select bibliography

Books

Baxter, Richard. *The Saints' Everlasting Rest*. Originally published in 1651. Many modern editions available.

Brooks, Thomas. *Heaven on Earth*. Edinburgh: The Banner of Truth Trust, 1983.

Bunyan, John. *The Pilgrim's Progress*. Originally published in 1678 and 1684. Many modern editions available.

Burroughs, Jeremiah. *The Rare Jewel of Christian Contentment*. Edinburgh: The Banner of Truth Trust, 1964.

Clarkson, Margaret. *Grace grows best in winter*. Grand Rapids: Eerdmans Publishing Co., 1984.

Cook, Faith. *Samuel Rutherford and his friends*. Edinburgh: The Banner of Truth Trust, 1992.

Cross, F. L. and E. A. Livingstone. *The Oxford Dictionary of the Christian Church*. Oxford: Oxford University Press, 1997.

Davis, Robert. *My Journey into Alzheimer's Disease*. Carol Stream: Tyndale House Publishers, 1989.

Davies, Eryl. *Heaven is a far better place*. Darlington: Evangelical Press, 1999.

Donnelly, Edward. *Biblical Teaching on the Doctrines of Heaven and Hell*. Edinburgh: The Banner of Truth Trust, 2001.

Edwards, Jonathan. *Charity and its Fruits*. Edinburgh: The Banner of Truth Trust, 1986.

Elliott, Charlotte. *Hours of Sorrow, Cheered and Comforted*. Religious Tract Society, no date, *c.* 1879.

Gilmore, John. *Probing Heaven: Key Questions on the Hereafter*. Grand Rapids: Baker Book House, 1989.

Havergal, Frances Ridley. *Like a River Glorious*. Rio, WI: The Havergal Trust, 2003.

Havergal, Maria V. G. *Memorials of Frances Ridley Havergal*. London: James Nisbet & Co., no date, *c.* 1880.

Hendriksen, William. *The Bible on the Life Hereafter*. Grand Rapids: Baker Book House, 1959.

Hoekema, Anthony A. *The Bible and the Future*. Grand Rapids: Eerdmans Publishing Co., 1979.

Houghton, Elsie. *Christian Hymn-writers*. Bridgend: Evangelical Press of Wales, 1982.

James, Sharon. *In trouble and in joy: Four women who lived for God*. Darlington: Evangelical Press, 2003.

Lewis, C. S. *The Problem of Pain*. New York: Macmillan, 1962.

Milne, Bruce. *The Message of Heaven and Hell*. Nottingham: Inter-Varsity Press, 2002.

Owen, John. *Works of John Owen*. Edinburgh: The Banner of Truth Trust, 1996.

Payson, Edward. *Legacy of a Legend*. Repr. Alabama: Solid Ground Christian Books, 2001.

Rutherford, Samuel. *Letters of Samuel Rutherford: A Selection*. Edinburgh: The Banner of Truth Trust, 1973.

Schenck, William. *Nearer Home: Comfort and Counsels for the Aged*. Stoke-on-Trent: Tentmaker Publications, 2003.

Smellie, Alexander. *Men of the Covenant*. Edinburgh: The Banner of Truth Trust, 1962.

Venema, Cornelis P. *The Promise of the Future*. Edinburgh: The Banner of Truth Trust, 2000.

Wiersbe, Warren W., ed. *Classic Sermons on Death and Dying*. Grand Rapids: Kregal Publications, 2000.

Other

'The Golden Age of Hymns.' *Christian History*. Issue 31, Vol. x, No. 3, 1991.

The Master Christian Library. Rio, WI: Ages Software, 2000. This CD contains many of the Christian classics of the past.

Hymnals

Christian Hymns. Bridgend: Evangelical Movement of Wales, 2004.

Praise! Darlington: Praise Trust, 2000.

Index

Aberdeen, 130-131

acceptance, 16

Alexander, James W., 94

Alzheimer's disease, 50-53

Ambrose, Bishop of
    Milan, 80

Anworth, 130-131, 135

assurance, 3, 10-12, 14, 16,
    32-33, 129

Augustine of Hippo, 80

Bavinck, Herman, 117

Baxter, Richard, 4-5, 117

Bedford, 70

Berkhof, Hendrikus, 114

Berthelsdorf, 10

Beveridge, Bishop, 48

Bonar, Andrew, 6, 56

Bonar, Horatius, 56-57

Bonar, Isabella, 6

Bonar, Jane, 56

Bradford, John, 66

Brainerd, David, 29

Brixham, 44

Bunyan, John, 70, 73

Burma, 81

Burns, William, 56

Calvinist, 76, 130

cancer, 28

Charles II, 70, 132

Chicago, 8

China, 28

Christian fellowship, v, 58

Christlikeness, 6-7, 23, 58

Church of England, 38, 54

Civil War, 70

Clarkson, Margaret, 16-17,
    24-25

Columba, 68-69

comfort of God's Word,
    26, 36, 38, 65, 72, 74, 85,
    91, 109-113

coming of the Lord, 9, 64,
    97, 102, 109

consumption, 76

Cousin, Anne Ross, xii,
    130, 138

Davis, Robert, 50, 53

delight in God, 4, 57

dependence on God, 3, 22,
    25, 29, 35, 40, 48, 54-55,
    63, 65, 68, 77, 78, 79

discouragement, 24, 82

disappointment, 26, 74

Donnelly Edward, 121

doubt, 3, 11, 70-73, 82

Dublin, 76

Dundee, 6

Edwards, Jonathan, 124-129

Elliott, Charlotte, xi, 82-83, 89

encouragement, 42, 89, 97, 117

England, 8, 70

eternity, v, 6-7, 22, 47, 48, 91, 95, 118, 121, 123, 124

exhaustion, 3, 24-25, 44

example of Christ, 87, 92, 93, 125, 129

facing death, 23, 28, 35, 38, 42, 46, 60-61, 62, 68, 70-73, 75, 79, 81, 84-85, 86-88, 89, 90-91, 92-94, 130-131

faith, 11, 17, 22, 23, 29, 38-41, 42, 60, 74, 121

faithfulness of God, 2, 14, 24, 28, 31, 32-33, 35, 36-37, 38, 54-55, 91, 123

Fawcett, John, v

fear, 11, 14, 23, 28, 51, 65, 68, 71, 78, 92

feeling overwhelmed, 12, 14, 23, 45, 65, 70-73

Flavel, John, 81

forgiveness, 11, 84-85, 93

Fortman, Edmund J., 118

friendship of God, 28, 35, 39, 45

fruitfulness, 31, 40

Gerhardt, Paul, 92, 94

glory, xii, 22, 128, 130-138

godliness, 41

grace, 5, 11, 14, 17, 23, 25, 31, 37, 40, 41, 42, 104

Great Awakening, 124

growing older, 31, 33, 34, 35, 37, 38-41, 42, 45, 47-49, 62

guilt, 11, 45, 71, 77

Havergal, Frances Ridley, 26-27, 84-85, 98, 100

healing, 16-17

heaven
    anticipating, 21, 27, 49, 60, 64, 76, 84, 86, 90, 98-100, 128, 130-138
    comfort of, 15, 22, 46, 47, 54-55, 77, 85, 94, 96, 103, 132
    entering, xii, 46, 71-73, 77, 81
    goal of, 9, 97
    hastening the day, 9, 60, 98, 128, 132
    joys of, xii, 4, 22, 53, 73, 81, 86, 97, 101, 102, 104, 111, 114-115, 117, 118-119, 124-129, 133-138
    meditating on, 4, 49, 64, 85, 89, 132
    new bodies, 21, 40, 60,

79, 81, 96, 101, 104,
106-108, 112-113
rewards, 121
seeing Christ, 35, 39, 42,
60, 72, 89, 91, 94, 97,
107, 121, 132
seeing one another, v,
116-117, 126-128

Hendriksen, William, 116
Herrnhut, 10
Hoekema, Anthony A.,
105, 108, 115
holiness, 6, 31, 76, 127
hope, 11, 21, 32, 39, 48, 61,
77, 88, 99, 100, 115, 117
illness, 3, 13, 22, 26, 28-29,
36, 38, 42, 47, 62, 65, 76,
81, 82, 89
imprisonment, 66, 70, 86,
130
Ireland, 76
joy, 10, 18-19, 25, 27, 29, 35,
45, 57, 72, 85, 89, 93, 100
judgement, 61, 76, 77, 80,
98, 102-103, 132
Judson, Adoniram, 81
Kenmure, Lady, 131
Kuhn, Isobel, 28-29
Kuyper, Abraham, 114
Lewis, C. S., 118
London, 54, 66, 130

loneliness, 20, 35
losing strength, 12, 15, 25,
26, 42, 62, 71, 132
love of God, 12, 16, 18-19, 23,
26, 42, 52, 53, 63, 85, 100,
118, 122-123, 124-129, 131
light of God, xii, 19, 57, 64,
85, 101, 124, 127
Lutheran, 92
Lyte, Henry F., 44, 46
Maclaren, Alexander, 86, 88
Manchester, 86
Matheson, George, 18-19
M'Cheyne, Robert Murray,
6-7, 56, 122-123
meditation, 4-5, 84
memory failing, 38, 47-49,
50-53
mercy, 5, 10-12, 20, 24, 43,
80, 88, 89
Milne, Bruce, 102-103
mission work, 10, 28, 68, 81
Montgomery, James, 90-91
Moravian, 10
new creation, 21, 96, 104-
105, 108, 109, 112-113, 114-
115, 118-119, 120-121
Newton, John, 74-75
Nonconformist, 54, 70
pain, 13, 14, 16-17, 18-19, 26,
38, 41, 42, 47, 66, 76, 91
patience, 26-27, 38, 41, 42, 100

Payson, Edward, 64

peace, 17, 26, 39, 41, 52, 73, 85, 88, 105, 128

persecution, 14, 23, 131

perspective, 5, 9, 21, 22, 48, 102, 109, 118, 131

Portland, 64

power/strength of God, 14, 15, 17, 23, 26, 31, 36, 42, 65, 75, 78, 94, 107, 122

praise, 20, 24, 32, 49, 67, 72-73, 76, 78, 102-103

prayer, 4-5, 16, 18, 20, 26, 28, 43, 44, 52, 76, 128-129

preciousness of Christ, 7, 23, 56-57, 76

presence of God, 14, 15, 18-19, 23, 25, 29, 35, 36-37, 42, 45-46, 60, 64, 65, 66-67, 71, 97, 101, 105, 117, 122, 124-129

promises of God, xiii, 3, 16, 19, 23, 33, 35, 36-37, 38, 42, 65, 66, 74, 85, 104, 110-111

providence, 23, 49

provision, 74-75, 77

punishment, 7, 61, 85, 102-103

Puritan, 81

purposes of God, 17, 23, 37, 79, 102, 104-105, 122-123

Queen Mary, 66

Romaine, William, 38, 41, 43

Rothe, Johann Andreas, 10, 12

Rutherford, Jean, 130-131

Rutherford, Samuel, 130-138

sacrifice of Christ, 11, 37, 76, 82-83, 93, 137

salvation
assurance of, 3, 11-12, 16, 23, 33

all of Christ, 75, 82, 84, 89, 91, 122-123

certainty of, 11, 25, 37, 39, 43, 61

doubting, 71

freely offered, xiii, 3, 57, 82-83, 131

fullness of, 9, 39, 67, 76, 123

history of, 109

proclaiming it, 6, 33, 104, 131

urgency of, 6-7, 131

Schenck, William, xi

Scotland, 6, 56, 130

separation from loved ones, 12, 35, 56, 61

separation of death, 35, 97

service to God, 58, 60, 79, 101, 115, 120-121
singing, 7, 67, 136
sleeplessness, 24-25
Smithfield, 66
sorrow, 9, 38, 56, 101, 111, 129, 130-131
sovereignty of God, 16, 23, 25, 32, 61
Spafford, Horatio G., 8-9
Spurgeon, Charles Haddon, 3, 62-63
St Andrews, 130
St Mary's College, 130
suffering, 16-17, 18, 20, 21, 25, 27, 41, 62, 131
Surrey, 76
temporariness of this world, 11, 46, 66, 79, 81, 87, 106-107, 112-113, 128
temptations, 5, 40, 45, 115
testing, 14, 71
Thailand, 28
thankfulness, 41, 43, 67, 87, 94
Thurneysen, Edward, 119
Toplady, Augustus Montague, 76-77
Tower of London, 66
trials, 9, 14, 18, 20, 22, 23, 24, 27, 34, 37, 62-63, 71, 78, 92, 132

trusting God, 3, 22, 25, 27, 31, 40, 57, 66-67, 68, 73, 78, 82, 85, 87
tuberculosis, 64
von Zinzendorf, Count Nicholas, 10
Vos, Geerhardus, 106
walking with God, 4, 32-33, 39, 40, 57
Watts, Isaac, 54-55
weakness, 3, 14, 26, 33, 38, 41, 42, 47, 63, 66, 75, 106, 132
weariness, 19, 24, 28, 57, 66
Wesley, John, 10, 12
Westminster Assembly, 130
will of God, 2, 16-17, 26, 42-43, 49, 87

Periodicals

Gospel Magazine, 76

Other works

By Searching, 28
Charity and its Fruits, 124
Expositions of Holy Scripture, 86
Hours of Sorrow Cheered and Comforted, xi
Lex Rex, 130, 132
Nearer Home: Comforts and

Counsels for the Aged, xi
Rippon's Selection (1787), 37
Scottish Psalter (1650), 65
The Pilgrim's Progress, 70
The Saints' Everlasting Rest,
    4-5
The Triumph of Faith, 38

Scripture references

GENESIS 25:8 39
DEUTERONOMY 33:27 62
JOB 7:3-4 24
JOB 19:26 107
JOB 23:10 14
PSALM 2:8 110
PSALM 8:4,6,9 120
PSALM 17:15 39
PSALM 23 65
PSALM 27:10 35
PSALM 30:5 25
PSALM 46:1-4,10-11 78
PSALM 71:1-9,17-18 33
PSALM 73:23-26 15
PSALM 77 24
PSALM 90:10 38
PSALM 92:12-15 31
PSALM 96:11-13 102
PSALM 110:1-2 109
PSALM 142:1-3,7 20
PROVERBS 16:31 31
PROVERBS 18:24 35

ECCLESIASTES 12:1-7 34, 38
ISAIAH 2:2-4 110
ISAIAH 11:6-9 111
ISAIAH 25:6-8 111
ISAIAH 26:3 73
ISAIAH 40:10 36
ISAIAH 41:10 36
ISAIAH 43:1-3 14, 36, 72
ISAIAH 46:4 31, 36
ISAIAH 60:20 XII
ISAIAH 65:17-25 112-113
ISAIAH 66:22-23 113
DANIEL 12:2-3 107
HABAKKUK 3:17-18 10
ZEPHANIAH 3:17 26
ZECHARIAH 14:7 XII
MATTHEW 8:11 117
MATTHEW 25:23 121
LUKE 13:28 117
LUKE 16:9 116
LUKE 23:43 61
JOHN 3:36 85
JOHN 6:35-40 2
JOHN 6:37 XIII, 3
JOHN 15:5 40
ACTS 3:19-21 104
ROMANS 8:18-23 21
ROMANS 8:28-39 23, 122
ROMANS 14:8 87
1 CORINTHIANS 13 124
1 CORINTHIANS 15:42-44
    106

1 Corinthians 15:50-58 79, 103

2 Corinthians 4:16 – 5:1 22

2 Corinthians 5:7-8 60

2 Corinthians 12:9-10 14

Ephesians 1:9-10 104

Ephesians 1:12 17

Ephesians 3:17-19 122

Philippians 1:21-24 60

Philippians 3:10 87

Philippians 3:20-21 107

Colossians 1:19-20 105

1 Thessalonians 4:13-18 97, 107

1 Thessalonians 4:17 90

2 Timothy 4:6-8 86

Hebrews 2:7-9 120

Hebrews 6:18 36

Hebrews 11:10 39

Hebrews 13:5 35, 36

1 Peter 2:24 85

1 Peter 4:19 17

1 Peter 5:7 35

2 Peter 3:12-13 104

Revelation 2:17 118

Revelation 4:3 128

Revelation 5:13 73

Revelation 6:9-10 61

Revelation 11:17-18 103

Revelation 14:13 60, 114

Revelation 19:9 71

Revelation 21;1-4 101, 120

Revelation 21:11 128

Revelation 21:24-26 114, 127

Revelation 22:1-5 101

Revelation 22:7 98

Revelation 22:12 98

Revelation 22:20 98

Other titles by
Sharon James

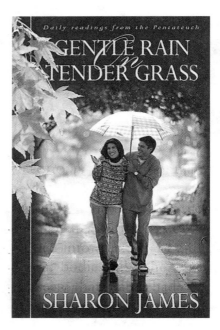

Gentle rain on tender grass
Daily readings from the Pentateuch

When Moses came to bid farewell to the people of Israel, he summarized God's message to them in a song, opening with the words: 'May my teaching drop as the rain … like gentle rain upon the tender grass.' Grass needs regular rainfall, not just the occasional torrent. And so it is with us. 'Gentle rain on tender grass' is a lovely picture of continual, persevering study of the Word of God. There is no substitute for exposing ourselves daily to God's own infallible, authoritative Word.

In a series of readings designed for daily devotions, Sharon James takes the reader through the first five books of the Bible. These five books are foundational to understanding the story of salvation as taught in the rest of the Bible. All the major themes are highlighted and at the end of each day's reading a verse of Scripture has been selected to help focus our thoughts on a particular truth throughout the day.

PPK 256 pages   ISBN   0 85234 630 1   ISBN-13   978 0 85234 630 3

www.evangelicalpress.org

In trouble and in joy
Four women who lived for God

In this book you will meet four remarkable women: Margaret Baxter, a rebellious, glamorous teenager who ended up falling in love with and marrying a Puritan minister twice her age; Sarah Edwards, whose spiritual experience during a time of revival has gone down as one of the most profound in church history; Anne Steele, who refused several offers of marriage, preferring to maintain her independence, and who had a significant ministry writing hymns; and, Frances Ridley Havergal, who was one of the most well known Christians in Victorian England because of her prolific writing of books, hymns, tracts and devotionals.

These four women knew that contentment and happiness did not depend on good health, a fulfilling job, or a happy family life. Through a selection of extracts from their writings you too can discover first-hand the heart for God that captivated these women and enabled them to live for his glory, whatever the cost.

PPK 288 pages ISBN 0 85234 584 4   ISBN-13 978 0 85234 584 9

www.evangelicalpress.org

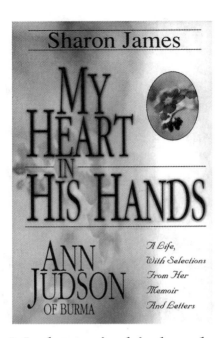

My heart in his hands
Ann Judson of Burma: a life with selections from her Memoir and letters

In October 1810, a twenty-year-old girl in the quiet New England town of Bradford wrote the following words in her journal: 'If nothing in providence appears to prevent, I must spend my days in a heathen land. I am a creature of God, and he has an undoubted right to do with me, as seems good in his sight... He has my heart in his hands, and when I am called to face danger, to pass through scenes of terror and distress, he can inspire me with fortitude, and enable me to trust in him. Jesus is faithful; his promises are precious. Were it not for these considerations, I should sink down with despair.'

Ann Hasseltine had received a proposal of marriage from Adoniram Judson, who was shortly to leave for Asia as one of America's first overseas missionaries. And thus commenced one of the greatest dramas of church history — a saga of love, courage, suffering and perseverance.

PPK 240 pages   ISBN   0 85234 421 X   ISBN-13   978 0 85234 421 7

www.evangelicalpress.org

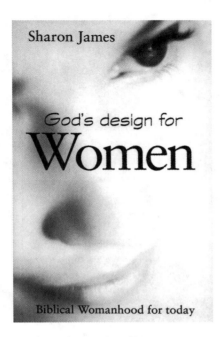

Sharon James

God's design for

Women

Biblical Womanhood for today

God's design for women
Biblical womanhood for today

Women today are encouraged to think they can 'have it all'; career success and family fulfilment at the same time. But these external measures of 'success' leave many feeling inadequate. Sharon James shows that every woman has dignity as she has been made in the image of God, and that every woman can find true fulfilment when she understands, enjoys and fulfils her creation design.

God's design for women has been written for:
- Christian woman who want positive biblical teaching on womanhood, including issues such as singleness, marriage, motherhood and workplace.
- Church leaders who want to encourage biblical women's ministries.
- Students and others who want a biblical perspective on modern feminism and women in ministry.

* *Questions for group discussion are provided.*

PPK 368 pages ISBN 0 85234 503 8 ISBN-13 978 0 85234 503 0

www.evangelicalpress.org

A wide range of excellent books on spiritual subjects is available from Evangelical Press. Please write to us for your free catalogue or contact us by e-mail.

Evangelical Press
Faverdale North, Darlington, DL3 0PH England
Evangelical Press USA
P. O. Box 825, Webster, NY 14580 USA
email: sales@evangelicalpress.org

www.evangelicalpress.org